I was listening to Dr. Tony Evans sermons one day. The title of the sermon is, "Your Time Is Now."[1] In this sermon I listened closely because it was about a woman who did not realize that God was using her for a time in history that prevented the annihilation of the Jews. Dr. Evans spoke about the fruits from the root of an issue that was not dealt with long ago, because King Saul was disobedient to what God commanded him to do. 1 Samuel 15 is where you can read about God's command and why Queen Esther and the Jews were facing annihilation. King Saul did not deal with the root; thus, the Jews were facing the fruit stemmed from the root that was not taken care of when God commanded King Saul to do so.

Because of my disobedience, I found myself with the fruit of the root of a problem that was not dealt with earlier. In my Dr. Tony Evans voice "Because I should have dealt with it, wished I would have dealt with it, I would not have been dealing with the issues I had to face the past three years. And, because I did not deal with it, when I should have dealt with it, I am now dealing with the fruit of the root. Even to this day I am dealing with the repercussions of unaddressed sin and disobedience."[2]

All of this was revealed to me when I listened to Dr. Evans sermon. Oh man, did it not cut me deep! I knew I needed to hear this message, because if I did not hear this message I do not know if I could have finished this book.

---

[1] https://youtu.be/2dQZj99IGm4

[2] https://youtu.be/2dQZj99IGm4

My time is now! It is my time to tell my story, to share with others the pain, anguish, dangers, sadness, and temporary defeat. It is also time to share my triumph and victory, by placing God's amazing grace on display by using my story for His glory.

Not too many of us will know what Ephesians 6:12 mean, unless we have come face to face with darkness and wickedness in high places. I mean, I have witnessed spiritual warfare, but never in any previous marriage in this way. The ESV of Ephesians 6:12 says, "For we do not wrestle against flesh and blood, but against the rulers, against the authorities, against the cosmic powers over this present darkness, against spiritual forces of evil in the heavenly places."

Dr. Tony Evans makes it clear when providing a metaphor for this passage of Scripture. "Spiritual warfare is the conflict in the spiritual realm that affects the physical realm. The demonic realm watches the film of our history, and they know our weaknesses and our sin pattern. They can use our sin pattern and history to prevent us from experiencing God's will for our lives."[3] It is easy for satan (no capitalization on purpose) to win in this battle when we do not know who we are in Jesus. When we do not exercise the power of His Word. It worked for Jesus when tempted by satan. Admittedly, we must know that it will work for us. The Apostle Paul tells us how we can fight against the schemes of the devil in the proceeding verses. Therefore!

If we know what and who we are battling against, why wouldn't we arm ourselves with God's armor, which is His Word and instructions, when we are facing spiritual warfare from within ourselves and others?

---

[3] Dr. Tony Evans, Tony Evans Bible Commentary, (Homan Bible Publishers) Nashville, TN. page 1232-1233

Acknowledgement & Book Dedication

I am no "Best Selling" author, and I will admit I am a novice at writing. This is my first attempt at writing something on this magnitude. Where I expose myself and unfortunately, it will expose other people in a not so enchanting manner.

The lies, deceit, narcissism, co-dependency, systemic racism I experienced. I write about these things because I fell prey to them all.

I am also sure there will be some backlash regarding the title of this book. "Who is she to say that PTSD is not mental, but spiritual." Well, this is my opinion, and by the many occurrences in the Bible, in which I hold firm to be as true, it gives many accounts of Jesus rebuking demonic spirits from those He encountered who were possessed with these spirits.

Writing this book was the hardest book to write, and if I should write another one, I pray that it is one of inspiration, hope, and encouragement. Maybe a thriller? Who knows? Often, I had to stop writing for weeks at a time because it was just too painful for me to re-live the horrible memories I endured in this marriage. My anxiety level was at one hundred percent and then some; it was important to me to take my time. Incandescent is an understatement!

This book is dedicated to the many spouses who have lost their lives due to domestic violence by those who clutch to PTSD, and for those who live in the presence of emotional, mental and physical abuse.

I pray that one day you will find the strength and realize that you are too valuable to stay in dangerous situations, that may cost you your life, and perhaps the lives of your children.

I ask that you take notice and start asking questions when your daughter seems to make excuses for not coming to family functions or make excuses for her husband's behavior.

Pay attention when your grandchildren are quiet and seem to be unhappy. When they seem to be jumpy at the sound of a loud noise, or a stern voice. When they go hide out at the sight of an argument or disagreement.

It is ok to seek help, get help, and to leave a dangerous situation. It is not ok to remain in a dangerous situation. It is ok to tell family what you are dealing with. It is not ok to remain silent.

To My Family and Friends

To my dearest London. My granddaughter, who had to experience Roger's rage and anger. I sincerely and deeply apologize. I pray that none of what you experienced on my selfish part will scar you and prevent you from living a fruitful and healthy life. You were my guardian angel throughout all of this, and I could never repay you for your wisdom and being an adult more so than Roger, and I could ever have been. Please forgive me for being blinded by the thought of love!

To my daughters, Shauna, Shemesha, and Selena, I pray that my terrible decisions will not have you believe that you are not worthy of true love and a man with integrity and Godly characteristics. You are all queens, and you deserve a man who will treat you as such. You do not deserve anything less.

To my son Stephen, you are such an inspiration to me. You are a wonderful father and provider to your sons. I admire you so very much. More than you will ever know. I pray that if God allows another man in my life, that he will possess your loving characteristics.

To my dear friend Brenda. Thank you so much for waking up in the middle of the night and taking my phone calls. I know we do not see each other, or talk to each other like we used to, but I just want you to know that I appreciate you and will always be here for you when you need me.

To my numerous friends and family who listened to me vent about this whole horror show of a marriage, I truly thank you for not judging me or saying, "I told you so."

Thank you for your prayers and words of encouragement. I know I could have talked to God about all what I was going through, but therefore, He gave us family and friends. We are to share in one another's suffering, burdens, and contribute to the healing process. You all rock!

To my Father in Heaven for comforting me, guiding me to all truths, being my provider, rebuking, reproofing, and restoring me in such a short time to a place I never thought would be possible. No one will ever be able to convince me that You are not the Creator of everything, and God of the universe with unyielding grace and mercy. Your love never ceases to amaze me.

Selah!

I want to let you know that this was very hard for me. To expose myself in this way. I pray that you will not think less of me for staying in a marriage where many of you had no idea of the trauma and abuse that I had endured.

More than likely, you will sense the bitterness and anger in my book. It is because when I started writing this book, I was very bitter and very angry! I prayed every day that God would remove this anger and bitterness from me.

I kept playing things over and over in my head. How did someone like me allow someone to come into my life to use and abuse me? Was I that desperate for a husband?

The enemy fled when he could not tempt Jesus, and if you have ever used God's Word to rebuke the devil, you would agree that it works. Only when we love chaos over peace would be a reason for us not to arm ourselves with God's armor.

I hate that I did not use God's truths as much as I should have during my marriage. There were times, and I might add, many times that my flesh got the best of me. As you read on, you will see that I was no match for the enemy. He almost devoured and killed me. But God!

First, I would like to acknowledge that I love our veterans, men, and women who wore and continue to wear the uniform. Their selfless sacrifice is something I do not take for granted. I am not intentionally trying to demean or demonize anyone for their illness. I am writing to share my experience and those whom I know who have been diagnosed with PTSD. The family members who are currently having or had similar experiences.

I can tell you I do not wish this on a friend, family member, and not even an enemy.

There are several books available about PTSD and how to heal, along with so many veteran organizations where a veteran can get the help he or she needs. The key to taking advantage of the many PTSD programs is the veteran must have the will to get better. They must continue in the plans, which consist of therapy, counseling, and support groups. I have often asked if all these experts who write these books, hold support groups, and provide therapy have data on the effectiveness of their programs and publications. I am willing to go out on a limb to say there is very little success if any. If it is, it is only temporary, and the positive change is minimal.

The purpose of my writing about my experiences is (1) to bring awareness to this horrible illness, (2) educate others of the dangers of marrying someone with PTSD when it goes untreated, or they are in denial, (3) shed light on this horrific illness in hopes that the VA will do something, (4) encourage those who have PTSD to get the help they need. Your family needs you to be whole, (5) the adverse effects PTSD unleashes on the spouse and children, (6) advocate for spouses, the help and support needed for them when they are in dangerous situations, (7) my answer to PTSD, God and Him alone (Psalms 51:10, Romans 12:2).

I cannot speak for all spouses who are married to a combat veteran who has PTSD, but I have read many comments of angry spouses who are tired of the behavior of their veteran spouse who has PTSD. I just know that my experience was, for the most part, outright horrific and debased! And I do not understand that level of horror that I experienced being married to a veteran that I am sure is more than PTSD. It is spiritual wickedness in the highest form!

My purpose is not only to shed light on my experience; it is my sincere prayer that my estranged ex-husband will cease from playing the victim, be honest with himself, as well as others that he is a very mentally ill man, and he needs help. I learned disturbing things about Roger, after our separation. The things I learned of what he had done to other women in previous relationships, I can truly say that I am so Blessed to be alive.

Some hard truths for Roger's family and friends who appease him because of fear and other reasons. By you continuing to turn a blind eye and appeasing Roger's behavior, remember, the things that Roger has done could be your sister, daughter, or someone you love.

Stop blaming other people for his behavior and encourage him to get the mental help he needs. I was amazed at your actions towards me when many of you have personally experienced this man's wrath and behavior. God forbid if this man ends up ending someone's life he is in a relationship with. And you all will say, "he did not seem like that type of person". Those people who really do not know Roger, that is to say. I suggest you Google "Narcissist", or for that matter, continue reading. I briefly discuss this type of personality. Pray that you will never encounter a malignant narcissist. The most dangerous narcissist, and the narcissist I was married to for three years.

Many people encountered this type of narcissist. Knowingly or unknowingly. Some were part of his demise by getting sent to prison because of his addiction, instead of owning up to his addiction and accepting the consequences, others paid a price with their freedom.

When we would go home to visit our families in Arkansas, people did not want to be around us. Especially, with Roger having a service dog. People thought it was a police dog and I often at times found myself explaining and telling people it was a service dog, and not a police dog. Still, people were skeptical. I learned why from Roger's own admission.

I recalled asking Roger about what some people were saying about him being a snitch. He assured me that he was not a snitch, that he worked with the police and he received a paycheck by working for them. He made it seem as though he was part of the police force drug unit. When he put it that way, I stood by him. Yes, I was very naive.

Now, I am not condoning anyone selling drugs to make money. I factually hate the fact that people who sell these hard drugs, who are not concerned about the lives they shatter, and the families they destroy.

Excuse me while I veer off the subject a minute or so.

Yes, I know if they do not do it, someone else will. Do the drug dealers ever think about the children who are left home alone due to an addicted mother chasing her next high? The stench and the filth of the dwelling place where these young babies and children must fend for themselves?

Going days without eating, dirty clothes. No running water, electricity, or gas in the home. Nothing but a cup of cereal, a couple of ketchup packages, mildewed bread, and outdated milk. Dishes piled high in the sink, dirty dishes in the bedroom, living room, and even the bathroom. The children must sleep on pee-soaked mattresses with no clean bedding, or perhaps on the floor where roaches and possibly rats nibble on their face while they have cried themselves asleep from hunger pains.

The children stripped from their homes because of their mother, father, or perhaps both of their drug addiction. Only to be placed in the system and handed over to strangers in foster care. The sleepless nights the children have because they are no longer with the family they so love. Perhaps, being molested by a foster parent who only see them as a means, to make money.

The children grow up bitter, angry, and find themselves walking in the same steps as their parent or parents. A never-ending vicious cycle. "I'm hurting, so we all have to hurt." God, help us!

I said I was going to veer off-topic for a minute, and so I did. Now back to the topic at hand.

Honestly, I confess to you that this marriage was very traumatic and, like nothing I have ever experienced in my life. I pray that my invisible wounds have healed, in so the next relationship I commit myself to, those wounds will not bleed on to him.

There have been a few events that have taken place since I began to write this book. I must acknowledge God; had it not been for Him hearing my cries, I do not know if I would have been able to hold on. Not by my strength, but only by God's power. I had to get prostrate a many of times, as Hannah did in the book of 1 Samuel. Whew Lord!

For seven days after I showered or bathed, I made sure that I had a white cloth on the floor, covering my head and praying to God to remove this pain of betrayal, lies, and deceit that pitted my most inner being. There were no words, just moaning and stillness. A few times, I cried out with a loud voice to God, saying to Him, "I am your daughter. I have been faithful to You, and You allowed this to happen to one of Your faithful servants. I know I am not perfect, but I do not deserve this. "HELP ME"! "VINDICATE ME"! "GET ME OUT OF THIS HOME"!

He did that, and so much more! God did. It is hard to explain, yet I was in a state of despair, anger, and bitterness. I still did not lose faith in God, but, yet I was also angry at Him. I knew He would deliver me, restore me, and set my feet on high places, but I did not know when. I did not want to go through that storm, as I had a glimpse of what I would have to endure. My prayer to God was that He would be with me through this category five storm that was upon me. I knew I would not be able to handle it without Him.

I knew it would be more pain than I could have imagined. It was!

God did not make this divorce easy for me. After being out of over six-thousand dollars for a divorce, simply because Roger did not honor my request when he first left in November last year. Initially I was upset since it was at my request that Roger file for the divorce, he did file. What I was so upset about is that his divorce petition was a total and complete lie. He claims there was no abuse, and we did not have any assets together. Ah, wrong! There was abuse, and there is certainly an issue with the 2019 Chevy Silverado that I signed my name to being the primary so that he would have something nice to drive.

The nerve of his attorney filing a contempt petition in court based on a lie. To say I was not following the court's order was a total and utterly pathetic lie. Roger's attorney wanted me to give him temporary power of attorney of my signature for the buyer of the truck. Apparently, the "buyer" did not trust me. After I found out who the buyer was, I realized the reason he did not trust me, is because what he had done to me. I would imagine if you have stepped on someone as if they were dirt, and you need for me to do something…yes, I could understand why you would not trust me. It was laughable and insulting at the same time.

I am not cut-throat like they are. I do not repay evil for evil. And as I stated to them, including my ex-husband before, God will repay.

Had Roger complied with my request of getting the truck refinanced in his name only, I would not have been out over six-thousand dollars.

And we both could have moved forward with our lives with almost a year gone by since he left. I was not having it and seeing that he was not making his truck payments on time, and many times being a month in the rear. I was getting insurance cancelation notices, so no sir, I was not signing off on this divorce.

Finally, we had a temporary court hearing in late September 2020. The Judge whom I could tell was not a friend of mine, although a woman, I knew Roger had been in contact with the court, being that he had often frequent Bartow County Courthouse for other veterans. Being that Bartow County is a "red" county, I am sure Roger made it known that I am no fan of corrupt Republicans.

Of course, he did not put it that way, but I am sure he did just as he did when I had to call the EMT to have a wellness check for his mental health almost two years ago. The first duplicitous act Roger did is when the EMTs and the police officers pulled up at the house. Roger came out shouting, "she didn't vote for Trump". As if he did. Wow!

This is the man I married. Someone willing to place their wife in harm's way to mask what they are trying to hide from public view. His addiction!

During the temporary hearing in September, I was glad the judge said my name must be removed from the truck, and Roger was given until December 31, 2020 to get it out my name. I was glad, but also disappointed that she gave him that long. I was ready to get this divorce over with, and expeditiously. I did not want to wait until 2021 to get a divorce. So, when all else fails, what do I do? That's right, I pray! A few days ago, around October 4th, I got on my knees and prayed to God. "Lord, I cannot do anything about this, but You can. Please help me get this divorce over. Bring this marriage to an end." God did that! On October 6th I received an email from my attorney with correspondence from Roger's attorney saying that he will be paying off the truck tomorrow and the bank will need to send the title to me. And when it comes, sign it and mail it to his office, and by doing this, we can we move forward with finalizing the divorce. But of course we can! This was the hands of God moving on my behalf and I was not going to make any other request. Let us put this puppy to bed! By answered prayers, I am finally free! The root has been cut off!

No one can ever convince me there is not a God. That Jesus is a fairy tale, or He is just a mere man. Miss me with that. I know Who I called on in my time of need.

So, in so going through this catastrophe, this was purposed for my higher calling in ministry. It is no coincidence that I went through all that I went through just to move on and keep my mouth shut. No, I had no idea women went through anything like this, and God was preparing me for such a time as this. It is no coincidence that I created my non-profit organization, Tears of Trauma Foundation, over three years ago. It is no coincidence that I have been educated and equipped to assist other women and provide services for this increasing demographic.

God has given me a fantastic opportunity to make a difference and be a voice for the voiceless. And His will shall be done!

It was October 9th, 2019, and I was out making sure our formal attire was on point with one another. The colors we chose were teal green to accent our black attire. Roger and I were so excited about our big night. It was the first time that we had been a part of something so amazing and beautiful. The Gala we hosted at the Fox Theatre in Atlanta, Georgia. We both put so much sweat, tears, and frustration into wanting it to be a success. Perhaps even a little blood, and I do mean literally, and not just metaphorically. I will write more on this a little later in the book.

That evening, we had packed our bags to head to downtown Atlanta to stay at the Georgia Terrace Hotel after the Gala. The next morning, October 10th, it was time to head out. I checked the house to make sure we had not left anything behind. The anxiety was at a hundred! I wondered if it was going to be a success and if people were going to show up. Worried that if people did not show up, it was going to look bad on my husband. Lord knows I did not want that to happen.

After Roger and I made it downtown, we begin helping the staff set-up and do a walkthrough to make sure everything was perfect. I was so proud of my husband. One of the Colonel's that were helping us, managed to get CBS46 to interview with my husband. He always wanted me by his side when he gave interviews. He said I kept him calm. For some reason, he did not give his best interview that day, but I was still proud of him. He was getting the message out to the public about the effects of combat-related PTSD and bringing awareness to those who are not familiar with PTSD.

After his interview, it was time for me to go to the room to get dressed. He had some things to tie up before he headed to the hotel to get dressed. By the time he made it to the hotel room, I was pretty much ready for our big night. It was my duty as his wife to make sure there was no hair out of place after he got dressed.

It was time! We stepped out of the hotel and walked across the street to greet the guest attending the Gala. Of course, we had to stop and take a picture of our awesomeness. As we walked into the ballroom, all eyes were on us! Roger went in a different direction to mingle with the guest and do what he does best. Be the life of the party. For me, I would share a smile with someone my eyes met looking at me. I also introduced myself to the Gold Star families that we had invited and honored during the Gala.

After a while, the ballroom had started filling up, and it was time for the ceremony to begin. Roger Bise, Jr., a known political figure in Georgia, told us during a few meetings we had before the Gala that he had gotten the Secretary of State to honor our Founder of the organization with a Georgian Honoree Citizenship. He communicated to us that he wanted to make sure Roger and I came upon the stage when he gave out the proclamation. What was a total shock to both Roger and me is that the reason Roger Bise, Jr. wanted us to come on stage to give the Founder the proclamation, is because he surprised us as well. Roger and I both received an "Outstanding Georgia Citizen" proclamation.

As soon as Roger Bise, Jr. said my name and read the proclamation, it took everything in me to hold back the tears. The tears did begin to flow. It was not because of receiving such a fantastic award, but because I knew in my heart that we were not deserving of such an accolade as that. The thoughts of what I had been going through with Roger up until the day before the Gala.
I want to take a step back and tell you about Roger Bise Jr., the compassion and kindness he showed me from the day I met him, and still, to this day. I am not sure if he will still feel the same after this book is published.

I was skeptical at first when I finally reached out to him about Roger, my husband. I did not know if he would be like the others and blow me off because I was a woman. Since the others whom I had tried to ask for help blew me off and acted as though I was of no importance. Roger Bise, Jr. did not do that. He gave me some great advice the first time I contacted him.

The award. On that stage I thought about the anger, the rage, the emotional, mental, and sometimes physical abuse Roger unleashed on me. We were just not worthy of such a proclamation. I knew it, and I am sure there were other people in attendance knew it as well. Who knew after this event, everything would start to take a down spiraling crash! For me, I should say. You would have thought that we would want to pattern our lives and live by the proclamation we had just received. I wanted that very much so. Unfortunately, my husband had other things in mind.

His crack addiction was more important to him and he was doing a great job at hiding it. It was more important to him than our marriage and unity.

Whenever my husband would come back from a crack binge, I would look at him in disgust—thinking about the filthy motel he had paid for to get high and wondering if it was some nasty skank accompanying him during those times. There was. I talked to a known drug addict about his withdrawals in the wee hours of the morning, and they assured me that the amount of money per night he was withdrawing, there was no way he could be smoking all by himself. If so, he would be dead. I am sure Roger's dealer loved seeing him coming to buy crack.

I am sure King David had PTSD, and in many of the Scriptures where we see him in action, we can tell that something is not right about his behavior. There is a difference in King David and many of our PTSD sufferers today… King David did not make excuses for his sin, and the things he did that were totally out of the will of God.

He owned up to his errors, repented of those things, and appealed to God. God loved King David so much, God stated it. It was not because of King David's works, but the zeal he had for God's righteousness. I wished that our veterans and those who have PTSD would diligently seek God. For if they did, PTSD would not hold them in bondage. They would realize they are free and can now live a life of liberty, joy, and purpose. Every day, I would hope and pray and often communicated to God that I wished my husband would have done this. Seek God. Do not just talk about Him, but diligently seek Him.

Being married to someone with PTSD is one of the most debilitating and unpleasant experiences I had endured in my life!

The foundation terminated my employment back in December of 2018, and my name poisoned like a venomous viper. Not only that, but there was also no money coming in, other than $335.00 per week from unemployment. Being stuck with paying rent of $1825.00 per month, utilities, car payment, and everything else to maintain me, and the home. Meanwhile, my husband has moved on to another woman. More on the other woman later. After receiving a change of address notification in the mail, I realized he had moved in with one of the veteran's that reports to him. I felt beyond betrayed! I gave all the support and love to this man, and this is the outcome of my loyalty to him.

Let's talk about narcissism, shall we? I did not realize this was my husband until he received the Director of Outreach position for the foundation over three years ago. Slowly, his narcissistic personality reared its ugly head.

Oh, how he loved to talk about himself, and what "he" was doing for the foundation. The Senators and Congressmen he had meetings with regarding what he was doing for veterans. Saving lives all by himself is what he boasted about the most. And his followers on FB, including me, were boosting his ego.

It was my job as his wife to support him administratively, and I also supported him financially. The new look with beautiful clothes, cologne, expensive watches, Cole Haan shoes, etc. I never believed he would turn on me as if I were the enemy by being a supportive wife. But he did, because apparently if you read about NPD (Narcissist Personality Disorder), that is what narcissists do. Once they have used you all up, and you are no longer a benefit to them, they will throw you away as if you are a piece of trash.

I read an article on the "Whatz Viral" website right after Roger did this. The title of the article is called "The Way Narcissist Gets Away with Hurting People and Come Off as a Good Person." I suppose that the article title did capture my attention, and one of the reasons I am citing it here! It described what I had just experienced with Roger. The author says, "They carry the dirty laundry while ensuring that nobody sees that the king is naked. So, it is tough to live in this world, which looks like it is created for and serves these manipulators. The author says they have multiple faces, and each one more deceitful than the previous. They can work a crowd and be so engaging and charming.

It is why everyone likes them, adores them, and feels as though the narcissist can do no wrong in their eyes of their peers. I thought to myself, "Wow, if this is not Roger." "This type of person has one target, which is the most compassionate person in the group. The article described me.

The author says the narcissist envies anyone better than them, and the compassionate, empathetic, and person with integrity becomes a threat that needs to be eliminated. So, the narcissist needs to dim this person's light and fast"![4]

"The target sees the true face of the narcissist but won't be able to do anything because they have too deep a connection with the narcissist. This person can be manipulated and abused by the narcissist". The narcissist is

---

[4] https://whatzviral.com/the-way-narcissist-gets-away-with-hurting-people-and-come-off-as-a-good-person/

very charming and charismatic, and others love them because this is the side outsiders only see. So, when they hear something negative about the narcissist, they find it hard to believe. After all, this person seemed to be such a wonderful person and is doing amazing things for the community. It is how they get away with doing horrible things to good people.

I talked to one of my sister's friends several months ago, and this is the first of her hearing what I had gone through with Roger. I told her that I could not believe how one of my sisters found Roger believable and not me. She said, "Bettye, Roger would come to your sister's house a lot of times and made it seemed as though you were such a villain, and he was the victim. And then you would come over and acted as though nothing was wrong." She said, "can't you see how your sister would believe Roger" You didn't say anything because you were trying to protect his image while he was destroying yours."

More on this later.

On November 27th of 2019, my life changed forever. On my way back from Virginia, an outreach trip for the organization I worked for, along beside my husband, I received a call almost an hour from home. My husband called me to let me know he had moved out, and more than likely, the Founder of the foundation was going to fire me because we would no longer be together. I was in shock, driving back from Virginia. My husband often threatened me with those words, "I will have you fired" for not complying to his demands of keeping his addiction a secret.

He often said that I would be fired whenever he came back from being on a crack binge. I realized this was a way to control me. If I reached out to anyone in the foundation to try and get help for him, in which I tried multiple times, Roger would always beat me to making that phone call to poison my name, so that if, and when I did try to reach out to get him some help, they would not believe me.

He made it seem like I was a jealous woman who always accused him of being with women or getting high. Oh, my goodness if they did not believe him. It was me giving him a hard time because he had PTSD, and I should take it easy. Be a Stepford wife, and comply with his demands. Unfortunately, this is not in my character. What kind of wife would I have been if I did not reach out to the organization, to get the help he desperately needed for his drug addiction?

When I met my husband almost three years ago, I never imagined I would experience the things I had endured during our strained three-year marriage. Yes, we got married way before we should have, according to society. I felt like I knew my husband because we are from the same area. And by many people telling me what a great and hard-working guy he is, including my ex-husband, I thought God had sent me someone who truly knew the meaning of love, commitment, loyalty, respect, and honesty.

When Roger, my husband, told me he had PTSD, I did not realize what PTSD exactly was. I had dated a guy who had PTSD a few years before beginning my relationship with Roger. And when I learned Roger had PTSD, I thought the symptoms would be concise to those of what my previous boyfriend went through, which was sleeping in the day and being awake at night.

They do not want to go out in crowded places and want the bedroom to be extremely dark. So, in my mind, and without doing any research, I thought this would be a breeze. I mean, Kirk, my previous boyfriend, was such a gentleman, easy-going, and a joy to be around. The pain was so enduring when we broke up because I never saw it coming. No explanation, just him saying he no longer wants to be in the relationship. I thought perhaps he felt like he was getting in too deep. In any case, it was a tough one to get over. We used to spend every waking moment on the phone or with one another.

He would drive over forty miles one way to pick me up to spend the night with him. I enjoyed going to his home, cooking him breakfast and dinner. It was something that brought me joy. Kirk introduced me to his parents and siblings, and he would even take me to family functions. I fell in love with his family. Especially his mom! I miss her, and I know she was fond of me and loved me too.

He knew that I was going to Seminary and respected the decision for wanting to wait until I was married before engaging in sexual intimacy. It was hard spending the night at his home in the same bed. It became a bit too much, unbearable even, and for the both of us. After a few months of dating, we engaged in sexual intercourse.

I did not want the relationship to end, and I tried to do everything I could to save our relationship. To no avail, Kirk was adamant about wanting to be single. I was heartbroken, and it took me a while to get over him. I do not think I got over him until he finally decided to meet with me to give me closure. Even then, it was hard to see him drive away.

Although we both said what we needed to say, Kirk was still such a gentleman, and he gave me a bottle of Angel perfume. He knew it was my favorite. And I gave him one of my books from Seminary by J. Dwight Pentecost, "Designed to Be Like Him, Understanding God's Plan for Fellowship, Conduct, Conflict, and Maturity." I hope that Kirk finds joy, happiness, peace, and love, or whatever will fill that void that he seems to be missing. Or, whatever he needs to heal so that one day he will be a great husband to someone someday. May he find that healing in God, first.

Roger's PTSD is very contrast to Kirk's PTSD. After learning about Roger's family history, and Kirk's family history, it is understandable that the symptoms are strikingly different. I will not get into that for now. There are significant variations of PTSD, and it is more severe based on one's childhood. Especially when one allows their childhood to hold them in bondage, and they cannot seem to live and let go.

This is my story about my life being married to someone with PTSD. In the pages to follow, I can only speak about my experiences and others I know personally in whom I have counseled or facilitated PTSD family support groups. Some of the names have changed to protect them.

What is it about me that I keep allowing the wrong men to come into my life only to destroy me? Is it them, or is it me? Perhaps both. I keep thinking about my daughters and the effect it has or will have on their decisions to be in a relationship with other men. I already see some things I know will not end well for them, but who am I to make their decisions when I have not been the role model they needed. I pray that my daughters will grow wiser than I ever did.

I thought about suicide a few times, as I knew what was to come during the healing process. Not wanting to face reality. Hoping this was all a bad dream and I would wake up with the marriage I always dreamed of. I did not want to face this. I was praying that it would not happen, but I knew it was bound to happen in the back of my mind. There was also something within me that would not allow me to quit and take my life.

Besides, I knew that with Roger's mentality, he would have probably not even come to the funeral and kept living his life as though he were the victim. Or, he would have milked as much sympathy from people as much as he could, had I decided to take my life. Roger would have been living his best life while I am waiting to be judged by God. Nah, I was not going to take that route. Bettye was not going out like a little bih, as the young folks say.

To be honest, I also had thoughts of homicide. I wanted to rid the world of Roger, and his side piece. When those thoughts surfaced, I immediately rebuked them in the name of Jesus. I will not be in prison, taking someone's life over events that were predestined. I will repeat Dr. Evans sermons that I mentioned earlier, "I wished I would have dealt with it, and if I had dealt with it, when I should have dealt with it, I would not be dealing with the issues I am dealing with today.

And because I did not deal with it, when I should have dealt with it, I am dealing with the fruit of its root".[5] I knew this happened because I disobeyed God, yet His grace and mercy saved me from this horror. This marriage should have never happened. Because of my faith in God and my fervent prayer, what the enemy meant for evil, God flipped it for my good. (Right now, somebody should be shouting, GLORY!)

I prayed for God to take this pain away, and I always prayed for God to change Roger, but to no avail. Things did not get better; they got worse. It was hard to keep a straight face and pretend to be the happiest couple, impacting, and changing lives. We needed the help more so than any support groups we facilitated, any presentation we gave, or any one-on-ones we conducted with other veterans and spouses or family members. Some people knew, but not many. I know from the look of the photos, we often posted being happy, it was far from the truth. It was like I was deceiving you all, leading you to believe we were living our best lives.

I know many people often thought I was so happy by things Roger and I posted. To my son Stephen there were times when I wanted to reach out to you and tell you what I was going through, but I just did not want you to worry, and I did not want to do that until the marriage was irreconcilable.

I recall a time where I had my phone getting ready to call my son when Roger was in his state of rage; he asked what I was going to do, and who was I calling. Let's just say

_____

[5] https://youtu.be/2dQZj99IGm4

that did not go over too well with Roger. I hate that I mentioned my son's name. He took my cell phone and left with it. Not before getting close to my face, spitting in my face and calling me every bad name he could utter.

One of my friends told me that this is one reason why some people did not believe me because I did not open my mouth while it was happening. That since I waited after the fact, I sound like some bitter woman making this all up. When I told her that anyone could ask my neighbors about the emotional and mental abuse, they heard Roger's rage and saw it first-hand, knowing I was not making anything up. If anyone Google's the number of times the police have been to our home, they will see that I am not making anything up. Our landlord experienced Roger's anger and rage on the telephone. So, there are several people who can confirm my claim.

How It All Began

It was my forty-ninth birthday, and that morning I woke up. I will never forget it. I had no clue what was in store for me.

I had just recently moved into a one-bedroom condo in Rockwall, Texas, and was at peace. No children, just me. My focus was on Seminary, work, and making good grades. On occasion, I would pick up my granddaughter London, and she would spend the night with me. More about London later. Just know that she is so wise to be ten now. Even then, she was only seven, but she has always been a gifted child. I can only accredit that to God.

On the morning of my birthday in 2016, I had logged on to Facebook. As usual, I knew people would be posting well wishes for my birthday on my page. Although there was one birthday post, I did not expect to see. I reviewed the notification from a name I recognized, but I knew we were not friends on Facebook. Roger Marshall Jr. sent me the sweetest birthday post with a Betty Boop meme.

I smiled once I saw that and thanked him anyway for the birthday post. After the response, Roger sent me a private message with his phone number. I told him I would call him later and told him to have a blessed day. Besides, I had planned a fabulous birthday outing for some family and friends. I had gone to the Christian bookstore earlier that week and bought some spiritual gifts for them and some other items. I wanted to be a giver on my birthday instead of receiving gifts. I was disappointed that my best friend, Brenda was not able to make it. Nevertheless, I enjoyed the few guests that did attend, including two of my beautiful daughters.

My oldest daughter lived in Arkansas at the time and could not make it.

We took a few pictures at the restaurant where I had made reservations for my birthday, and we enjoyed being silly.

Although the food was not good at all and came highly recommended by someone who previously worked with me, it was apparent, he has no taste in good food at all. It was horrible yet expensive. I was hoping that Kirk would walk through the doors and surprise me while at the restaurant. After posting my birthday pictures on Facebook, one of my guests was also a friend of Kirk's sister on Facebook. Kirk's mom used her daughter's account to see the happenings on Facebook, and when she saw my birthday post with LaDonna tagged on it, she commented on it, wished me a happy birthday, and told me that she missed me. I thought she was going to be my mother-in-law.

The night was over, I was looking so good, but there was still a void in my heart. I thanked my guest and my daughters for coming, kissed them all good-bye, only to go home and go to bed. I still thanked God for allowing me to see another birthday.

I cannot say that I was ecstatic that Roger had contacted me and provided his phone number. It was a kind gesture though, which is a reason why I did not immediately call him back. I believe it took me a few weeks before I called him. When I finally called him, he answered and asked if he could call me right back, because he and some other guys were getting something to eat. I later learned that he was so excited that I called him back. So, after getting back to the facility he lived at, he called me back.

One of the first things he said was, "First, I want to say this. I have no ill intentions or hidden agendas for reaching out to you, and I just want to see if I could get to know you." He asked if I was seeing anyone, and I asked the same. It would have been cool if he were because we were not on the phone to start a committed relationship right off the bat. We did not talk that long on the first call, but I did enjoy the conversation. Something that caught my attention when I first spoke to Roger, and it was his voice that had me interested to know more about him.

I could tell that he was intelligent, and I truly believed his heart was sincere. And although we were interrupted by some of the other veterans at the facility, where he was a mentor; I was okay with it because they often told one another, "I love you, bro." I thought what a great person, especially a black man, who can publicly say to another man, they love them. I felt as though if he tells them this, this must be a great guy.

Roger told me his daily routine. He would get up every morning at 4:45 AM to pray, meditate, and listen to gospel music. Roger's morning routine got my attention. I am sure he knew what kind of woman he was dealing with when it comes to me. I learned from him later that he had been researching me months before approaching me. Is not this how animals do their prey, before they attack, and rip them into pieces. Unfortunately, I did not question the fact that he was surveilling me like a thief does before they break into a house and steal all the homeowner's valuables.

At the time, I thought he wanted to be careful about who he gave his heart to, and wanted to be sure before approaching me.

As we became a couple, I can recall the commitment we made to one another when we first started talking. We both said that if we ever got to a place where if we got in a disagreement with one another, one of us would say, "Meet me in Heaven."

This meant that we would join in the Spirit of Christ, and immediately admit when one of us were wrong and pattern our behavior towards one another as Christ would have us to do. We would exercise the fruit of the Spirit instead of our flesh selfishness, where we would be able to resolve our conflict peaceably and agreeably. Roger used this method a few times, and I do not ever recall using it. The thought of resolving conflict in a Christ-like manner dissipated.

He had told his sisters about me and his counselor in Houston, Farah, about me. Not to mention all the guys at Camp Hope, which is the facility where he mentored the new residence in the program, and where he also resided. So, he had the upper hand. He had done his homework. As I think about it, it is kind of spooky.

After our first conversation, we became friends on Facebook. We would send each other encouraging messages and "like" or "comment" on one another's post. Every morning after that, he would text me good morning, or I would text him good morning.

It would be to see which one of us would be awake first. I would respect Roger enough to not interfere with his morning routine, and he would respect me not to call when I was studying or doing homework. It was refreshing and pleasant. We had numerous conversations throughout the day.

Roger would call me to let me know about his day, and I would tell him about mine. Nothing out of the ordinary, just really getting to know one another. Every night before we got off the phone with one another, Roger would pray for us.

Almost every time we were on the phone, we would get briefly interrupted by one of the guys at the facility. I could hear the conversations, and I could tell they always wanted to be around Roger. I could see why, and it was because Roger seemed to genuinely love those guys, and he was there for them. Whatever they needed, or wherever they needed to go, he would be there for them.

We decided on a date we would connect in person. Roger agreed to request time away from Camp Hope for Thanksgiving in 2017. He would come to Rockwall, stay a few days, have dinner with my family, and head back to Camp Hope. We were so excited about meeting one another in person, and the excitement overshadowed anything else we talked about on the phone.

Finally, it was time for him to take off driving from Houston to Rockwall. I stayed on the phone with him most of the time to make sure he was not sleepy. Although I was, I wanted to ensure his safety. When I heard the tires on his truck make a sound as if he were veering off the highway, I would ask him if he was okay. It seemed as though it took Roger forever to get to my home. Finally, he made it through the security gate, then to the visitor's parking space. I ran up the stairs to greet him. Roger got out of his truck and greeted me with an endearing hug. I helped him with his bags and brought them into the condo and showed him around my small one-bedroom condo. We both were so tired, but we stayed up talking and being intimate. No sex, but close. By the time we fell asleep, it was almost time for me to get up and make the food I took to my sister's home for Thanksgiving dinner. We both got up, had coffee, and talked while I was making my famous dressing. Roger would try to sneak and snap a photo of me while I was preparing the food. He was acting silly. Everything felt real and fantastic.

After I had cooked, we finally made it to my sister's home for Thanksgiving. I believe everyone was so eager to meet Roger, as I talked about him to my family before coming.

It was strange that Roger and my sister's boyfriend had on almost identical clothing. Of course, I have this one niece, Brooklyn, who is the life of any gathering or party. She made fun of them both. Of course, she was the person who questioned Roger as though he had committed a crime and was on trial. She drilled him to the max, so much so that I wanted to rescue him. The one thing that stood out to me in my niece questioning Roger was, "What if your PTSD got out of control"? Roger answered that it would not, because he has Jesus in his life and he had been delivered from the effects of PTSD. And as you read on, Jesus has determined that this was a lie. After our dinner with my family, we left and stopped by one of Roger's acquaintance's home. He found out they also lived in Rockwall. It was one of the veterans who had graduated from Camp Hope. We visited with them for a while and came home.

The next morning, I got up and made breakfast, and after we ate breakfast, Roger wanted to go to the lake. We got dressed and headed out the door. We stopped at the grocery store before making it to the lake. Roger said he needed to buy something. When he came back to the truck, he had bought me a dozen red roses. I was surprised, and it made me happy that he would be so thoughtful, and it was kind of romantic even. We finally made it to one part of the lake. It was on a fresh and crisp Friday morning. The sunrise was so beautiful, and the lake was still. Roger loved to fish, so of course, he had a fishing rod readily available. He threw his rod in a few times and snapped some photos of the both of us. He did not get a bite, so we got back in the truck and went back to the condo.

Saturday, we did not do anything; we hung around the condo, and since a part of Lake Ray Hubbard was within walking distance of my condo, we walked down to the lake so that Roger could get a look at it. Sunday was what I was looking forward to; we went to church.

I have always wanted to worship with someone I am in a relationship with. There is nothing more important to me than that. I could not wait to worship God together with Roger. I wanted to see if he was really into God as much as I was.

He made a first good impression by paying attention to what the Pastor was saying. There were sometimes during church service, where Roger felt the need to fidget around with his cell phone. Look on Facebook and scroll throw his newsfeed. I thought that was unacceptable during church service, but I did not say anything to him. I thought, maybe he was nervous, and this was his way of calming his nerves. Until I realized during our marriage and the numerous times we went to church, he would instead scroll through Facebook than listen to the Word of God. And it was during our marriage when he did this, that I would give him the side-eye. He would see me giving him that look and put his phone away for a few minutes. Being on social media is a pet peeve of mine. I cannot stand it when people are in church on Facebook or any other social media site.

We are in church to worship and give God praise, some of our time, and for spiritual growth. If this is not the goal, then we need to stay at home. Unfortunately, I do not believe this was Roger's goal. Perhaps it was to appease me, or maybe he was trying, but the enemy may have gotten the best of him where he would eventually give in totally to the enemy.

One of the first gifts that I bought Roger was an ESV Study Bible. And out of the many things I bought him, it is the one gift that he did not take with him when he left in late November of 2019. So, this lets me know who he was an agent for, and it did not appear to be God. I do not recall seeing Roger ever reading it. It now sits on my desk in my home office for me to utilize. I figured I would not allow it to go to waste. So, as I continue my studies attending Seminary, I often use it.

It was time for Roger to head back to Camp Hope in Houston. We both dreaded for that day to come when he had to go back to Houston. We did not know when we were going to see each other again. I believe we were shooting for Christmas, and we were going to go to our hometown, in Arkansas, to visit with our family. We talked to each other on the phone while he drove back to Houston. Talks about the future and how long he was planning on being at Camp Hope before moving off the facility. It was almost December, and the plan was for him to stay for another six months at Camp Hope. He would then get his own place in Houston.

It was about three days later when I received a surprise call from Roger telling me that he missed me so much; he had packed his truck up and asked if I wanted him to come and move in with me. It caught me off guard, and stupid me did not have time to process what was going on, so I said yes.

Roger was so persistent, well, what I know about him so well is that he was manipulative. Leading me to believe he missed me that much that he did not want to wait six months until we were formally together. And the way my heart is, I believed him.

It was December 4, 2017, when Roger moved in with me. I remember him saying all I have is about $400.00 to give you for rent. After this month, I will pay the rent for you, is what Roger said to me. I never really thought about why Roger only had about $400.00 to his name on December 4, when he just received his VA Disability check and SSI check, which was more than $4000.00. I realized later when I found out about his addiction as to why he only had about $400.00, and it was because he never stopped smoking crack. Yes, Roger had a truck payment of a little over $400.00 and insurance which was no more than $200.00. He had no mortgage or rent because he lived at Camp Hope free of charge. The food there was free, and it was plentiful.

Something was not right about this, to only have $400.00 from over $3900.00 and it was only December 4th. Not only that, Roger overdraft on his bank account for the $400.00 he gave me. I brushed it off and allowed Roger to move in with me.

Divineness?

I want to take you back a few years, 2013. Since I am a believer in God, follow Christ to the best of my ability, and if you are a follower of Christ and listen to the Holy Spirit, this will not sound strange. Roger and I both were mutual friends on Facebook with one of his relatives and his wife. I knew them very well, and I loved their marriage. They would take these awesome trips on the weekends just to eat at places that were on Food Network. I would comment on their post, and I notice this guy named Roger Marshall Jr. would chime in. One day he had made a comment, and I looked at his profile picture and thought, "Nah," he is not my type. The Holy Spirit said to me, "One day, he will be your husband." I was like, "no, he is not; he looks mean." Every so often, I would look at his profile, trying to find something that I would like about him, but I could not find anything. After a while, I just forgot about it.

If you think that is weird, how about this. Roger told me, or I should say, he reminded me that we were both in a youth shelter in Magnolia, Arkansas. My sister and I were there. We were taken away from our dad's home due to neglect and abuse. Roger was there because he was in a fight at school and used a hair pick on the person he fought. He told me about how we would sit on the floor in the common area and watch movies. According to Roger, there was this time while we watched a movie, Roger told me he whispered in my ear and said to me that I was going to be his wife one day. He used to tell people in our circle and when he gave presentations this story, and I did as well. How was it our marriage was in such chaos when we have waited for almost forty years to be married? I just did not get it.

Another experience. When we began our road to marriage, Roger moved to Rockwall, Texas, and moved in with me. More on that later. We were shopping for wedding rings and went to Zales. Since Roger loves to talk and was displaying so much affection towards me, the sales lady, inspired by our love, said she got goosebumps. She said, "That has never happened to me." She believed there was something special about our relationship. It gave me some comfort in thinking I was doing the right thing. How could all these experiences be happening if it were not God who was orchestrating our union?

One more experience, which got me to believe that everything was going to be okay, and we were great for each other. The day we got married by Rev. Aliene Bodholdt in Denton, Texas, she stated that she had this overwhelming feeling and got goosebumps also when she married us.

Although there were some challenges when Roger moved in with me, I felt that it was the enemy not wanting us to be married because we both seem to be going in the same direction.

We both have a desire to help other people who are hurting, and it just felt good knowing that we would be in the same type of ministry. Roger was assisting veterans in finding their way out of the darkness, and I was helping women to heal from past hurt and pain.

I thought once we got married, everything would go according to our plans. But was it God's plan? Yes, and no. What I mean by that is, even though the decisions we make, God already knows what we are going to do. We often take a detour by being disobedient to Him, and sometimes it takes us longer to reach our destiny because we chose to take a detour.

I remember praying to God that if this were not what He wanted us to do, let us get in a car accident so we would not be able to go through with it.

The Good Times

Where do I begin? The most memorable moments were before we got married. We had a favorite spot that we went to for a date. It was the TA Center where truckers go to park their rigs, shower, and sleep. We went there often, in his Ford F-150, to buy a cheap cup of coffee, and take turns playing our favorite songs to one another. We did this because money was tight. I can honestly say those were the best dates that I ever had. We were so in love with one another. It brings tears to my eyes, that love we had for one another back then, which was not long ago, has turned into something close to disgust and hate.

I was working when Roger first moved in, but after a few months, my contract ended. Roger VA benefits would only come once per month. At the first of the month, Roger would pay the rent; he would go to the store early in the morning and buy me little cute cheap gifts from Wal-Mart. Before the money ran out for the month, we would go and get Starbucks early in the morning or in the evening, and we would go to the top of this fantastic hill in Rockwall, Texas, to watch the sun hit Lake Ray Hubbard. It would be a great view in the evenings! It was as if God said to us, "This is for you two love birds."

Roger loves to fish, and he made this known when we first started talking on the phone. Once I looked at his Facebook page, I knew he was a serious fisherman. Fishing was his peace and way of escape from the demons in his head. After my contract ended with the company I worked for, I would often join Roger at Lake Ray Hubbard to fish. He and I would bet each other who would catch the first fish or catch the most fish. I would win sometimes, but most of the time, he would win.

There were times when we both were defeated by not catching anything. I showed him another spot, and it was another part of the lake we went to the day we got married.

We filmed a video of it. It was such a beautiful brisk evening after our ceremony. There is nothing like the stunning views at Lake Ray Hubbard. Spending time with Roger at the lake, those times were beautiful memories we shared.

I moved to Cumming, Georgia in June of 2017 to start a new position. For those of you who have never heard of Cumming, Georgia, it is about thirty-eight miles North of Atlanta. I had just got offered a good-paying job. Roger had left and gone to Houston. He needed to go and get some psychiatric treatment at a hospital in Houston, Texas. Roger became suicidal and angry at minor things. I remember him calling me telling me he was at a park with a rifle thinking about killing himself. I got on the phone with the VA hotline and told the operator about his call. I was scared when Roger stopped answering the phone. I tried to call him a few times for a few days, no answer. A few days later, I get a call from Roger telling me what happened. The police were dispatched to his location by his phone number, and the police officer took him to a mental hospital.

Roger was in the hospital for two weeks. Every day he would call me, and there were times when I would be on the phone having a counseling session with his counselor at the hospital. Roger blamed me for his mental state. More on that later, as this chapter is about the good times we shared. After Roger got out of the hospital in Houston, he called me and told me that he was going to spend the night at one of his friends' places in Houston.

We had planned to meet each other just to visit with one another at a half-point; we decided that it would be

Jackson, Mississippi. I believe we were both so eager for that weekend to come so that we could finally see and hold one another. I could not wait to get to Jackson, and neither could he. Roger made it to the designated destination we decided on before I did.

The anticipation of getting to him was unbelievable, and as soon as I parked my Juke behind his Ford F-150, we met each other with the biggest hug and kiss. We immediately found a nice Comfort Inn hotel in Jackson so that we could explore our love intimately for one another, and it was if we had picked up where we left off when things were good. We found a church to go to while we were in Jackson, and after church, we looked at some written reviews of a soul food restaurant and went there to enjoy some good ole soul food. We took pictures and posted them on our Facebook page, as though we were love birds for real. Back then, we were.

Roger surprised me to say that he was moving to Georgia as well. We did not have a clue as to where we were going to live. When you want your marriage to work and love one another, we could have lived in our vehicles, which would have been okay with me. Roger was not having it, though. I had not gotten paid yet, but he had money from his VA benefits. We pulled over in the wee hours of the morning at a gas station; Roger got on the phone and called Dobbins AFB, where they had a room for us. We stayed there for a few days, due to the base being full and a military exercise where active duty took precedence over non-active duty, so we had to break the days up staying at a different hotel. We had some points from Choice Hotels, so we moved to a Comfort Inn in Alpharetta Ga, and from there, we stayed at one in Duluth Ga.

We were back and forth, staying at different hotels. During the day, Roger would be on the phone with some veteran organizations in hopes of getting us some financial assistance. He was not going to let his family go without food and shelter. I can recall being frustrated with our living arrangements, but Roger was not having it. He stepped up to the plate and gave me a great pep talk. I loved this about him. He was indeed my king at the time I needed him to be. He allowed me to do my work and my homework while ensuring we had a place to lay our heads and food to eat.

If we had to switch hotel's we would hang out in a parking lot where we could find shade from the scorching sun. There were times when we would go to a park to eat and hang out until it was time for us to check-in the hotel. While I would work, Roger and London would play around until they got tired. We would pack up the food and drinks and head out and on to our next adventure.

One day we were on our way back from looking at a home one of my sisters was having built, and she saw this "For Rent" sign in a nearby subdivision. I entered the phone number in my phone and called the owner of the home. He agreed to meet us so that we could look in the inside of the house. It was more than what we needed, but we were desperate to find a place. He agreed to rent it to us. Although our credit was not stellar, he took a chance on us. I used my whole paycheck to pay the deposit. We were expecting a settlement from one of the hotels we were in litigation with, and once we received that check, we used that for part of the rent. A charitable organization helped us pay the rest of the rent.

The same organization that helped us pay part of the rent was the same organization that filled our home with furniture, some dishes, and linen. We felt so Blessed to be able to receive those items. We did not care that the items were used. I remember us sitting in the backyard on one of the lawn-chairs the landlord left. I was nestled in Roger's arms, and we thanked God for our Blessing.

Every morning after that, Roger was up early with the gospel music playing, a few hours before I opened my eyes. He would have already prayed for us. He even found a place where he could attend AA meetings. Although his problem was not alcohol, it was crack cocaine. He said the reason he liked going to AA meetings was because of how they conduct the meetings. I was a bit insecure, and the trust had somewhat gotten lost between Roger and me. Yet, he would put my mind at ease and let me know what he was doing and where he was going. I was expecting the expected. In hindsight, I wished I would have just prayed about everything that gave me that uneasy feeling. More on that later.

When it was time for grocery shopping, Roger would have already gone to the grocery store, bought small gifts for London and me, and by the time he thought I was up, he would bring me coffee in bed. I would make us breakfast, lunch, and dinner. He would make sure London had her favorites for her school lunch. Roger enjoyed making London's lunch every morning to make sure she had a balanced meal, and all that she needed to be satisfied at school. It was great to see him enjoying London with us as much as I was.

I will never forget the day London brought home the announcement for the "Daddy & Daughter dance." It was a 50's dress theme, and I immediately went to work to ensure Roger and London were well coordinated and one of the best dressed couples at the event.

I believe Roger was more excited than I was. Especially the evening of the event. It was cold, but the cold did not stop them from looking so magically wonderful. No expense was spared, and whatever it took to bring out the 50's in their dress, I did that!

Once Roger and London got dressed, I snapped so many photos of the two of them because I knew it would be something to look back and remember how wonderful things were.

I can remember Roger calling London to one of the dining room chairs making her close her eyes so that he could present her with a bouquet of flowers. I streamed it on FaceBook because I was so overjoyed by that moment and wanted everyone to see how wonderful they looked.

Once they made it to the event, Roger made sure he kept me abreast with what was going on. It was so much laughter and fun. One of the pictures Roger captured and sent to me of him and London holding hands, while she was looking up to him and he was looking down at her, is one picture I will never forget. I thought it really meant that he deeply loved her, and he would always be there for London. That was a beautiful picture, and regardless of what has happened, it is a picture that I will more than likely not part with.

All the joys and love that we were unleashing on one another, I thought, finally, our family was stable, we were committed, and there was a sense of hope. I had bought a book by Dr. Tony Evans titled "Kingdom Family." It is a devotional where we all participated in reading it at the dinner table. Even London participated. It was terrific, and we knew that God was with us.

The trips we would take to our favorite spot with Zapp, Roger's service dog, were memorable. Sometimes we took London with us, and there were times we had a married couple watch London, they had a daughter London's age. One of our favorite places to go was St. Simons Island in Georgia. We both shared the same sentiments that it was sheer serenity when we went there for a weekend or a long weekend getaway. We found this excellent restaurant called the "Half-Shell" that we would frequent when we went to St. Simons. They had the best oysters there. There is only one dessert they serve there, and it indeed is the only one they need to serve. It is amazingly delicious!

In speaking with Roger in April 2020, he disclosed to me that he took Karmai (the other woman) to our favorite spot, St. Simons Island. It is now no longer one of my favorite places. What an evil and vile thing to do. Later, on this.

Even after moving to Georgia, where we only had one another to rely on, it was those moments that made our marriage seem unbreakable. I can recall telling Roger this very thing, not too long ago before he left, that it was those times when we were closer together. Again, things changed when he got the position he now holds. There is something about power and prestige that diverts people from doing the right thing and their purpose. When Roger first got the position with the previous foundation, he told me that if the job, people, or family ever got in the way of our marriage, he would choose his marriage over anything or anyone else. I see now; this was the farthest thing from the truth, and our reality.

Roger immediately endowed me with compliments, encouragement, and some great memories initially. There were even some short-lived good moments we shared, and those moments gave me hope.

Why Do Spouses Keep Silent? Battered Woman Syndrome?

According to an article online by "Healthline," "Battered women syndrome" is caused by sustained and serious domestic abuse."
There is a predictable cycle, and they list that:

- The abuser will win over the new partner, often moving quickly into a relationship with tactics like "love-bombing," grand romantic gestures, and pressuring for commitment early.
- The abuser will be emotionally or physically abusive. The abuse often starts small, like a slap instead of a punch, or punching the wall next to their partner's head.
- The abuser will feel guilty, swearing they will never do it again, and be overtly romantic to win their partner over.

There will be a temporary "honeymoon" period, where the abuser is on their best behavior, luring their partner into thinking that they are safe, and things really will be different. Abuse occurs, starting the cycle all over again.[6] The above points are precisely the things I endured with Roger.

It would always seem to be this vicious cycle, over, and over again. And towards the end, it had gotten from a threatening phase to the physical hitting phase. Although Roger reframed from the visible physical abuse, the two times he hit me, it was head-to-head, a head butt. Of course, there was the one time where I lied about him messing up my left eye.

---

[6] https://www.healthline.com/health/battered-woman-syndrome#how-it-develops

Roger had just come back from a crack binge that night. I was already in my car, ready to pull off when he came to my car, telling me to roll the window down. Stupid me rolled the window down. If I did not comply, he would always say he would break it. And I did not want that to happen. He yelled obscenities at me, and at some point, he used his pointer finger as though he was going to press it against my forehead.

I moved, and his fingernail caught the bottom of the inside of my eyelid. All I saw at that moment was light. I tried to focus my left eye to see, and then I felt this liquid coming out of my eye fast and furious. I initially thought that he had poked a hole in my eye. I got out of the car and rushed into the house. Roger saw my eye, and the first thing he said was, "Oh shit, my life is over" after thinking about himself first, he then showed concerned about my eye. He abrasively said, "come here and let me see," I did not try to do that to your eye."

Why was I feeling bad for him? I cannot understand it. He encouraged me to go to the optometrist to get my eye checked out. The next day I made an appointment, and they quickly got me in. Of course, I lied about what happened. I told the optometrist that Roger and I were playing in bed, and he accidentally poked me in my eye. I do not know if he bought it, but that was the story I gave to protect my husband. The doctor made sure there was nothing I should be worried about, and he prescribed two prescriptions for my eye. One was an antibiotic, and the other one was a steroid for my eye.

Roger made sure he gave me the medicines on time every day. He said it was hard for him to look at me, and he was so upset with himself for doing that to me. When it initially happened, I would not leave the house, and if I did, I wore shades. I did not go around my sister until after my eye had healed. Even to this day, a flash of light will come across my left eye. I hope and pray that this will not have a delayed effect on my sight.

For me keeping silent, it was the sheer shame of being in another failed marriage. I was embarrassed, maybe. I am a Woman of God and look at what I have gotten myself in, yet again. What would my friends and family think about me? And if I did tell them, and stayed with Roger, they would not like him at all.

I did not want my family to know all the horrors I went through with Roger, although my daughters saw a glimpse of his anger. For example, when I did not want him to tell my daughters about his past. I thought it was best if he did not talk about his history to them. I was afraid they would not accept him and would judge him.

The horrors are so many other women truths who are married to veterans with PTSD. They do not want their family to know what they are going through. Or they will not let their family and friends know all the horrors they endure. It is embarrassing, and this is the reason some families end up dead due to murder-suicide. The family and friends are surprised because they thought the couple was happily married, and there were no signs of any abuse they knew about in the marriage.

I realize that many people will be angry at me for saying this, and perhaps even a target for writing this book. Again, my reason for writing this book is not to shame anyone, but it is my hope that the VA will begin to evaluate their care for veterans who have PTSD for the spouses who are causing chaos in their family's lives to get the help they really need. To be brutally honest, and in my humble opinion, God is the only answer.

And, of course the other reason is to bring awareness that it is not just the veterans who suffer, but also the spouses.

Rebellion, Discourse, and Madness

I will never forget that day when my middle daughter, Shemesha, was talking about her job. She worked for a company in Dallas, Texas, that sold telecommunication services to prisons. Roger started to talk about him remembering those times when he had to use the service when he was in jail. I tried to quiet him, and this was the wrong thing to do. He got so upset with me for not wanting him to talk about this in front of my daughter. He started yelling and cussing at me, "Bitch, who do you think you are?" Your kids know what's up. Just because your ass think you are holy than thou, do not mean your kids are like you".

Roger seemed to enjoy talking about his lawlessness. It made him feel like he could not be touched, due to some of the things he had gotten away with, and he often bragged about it. There were times when he would say to me, "BettyeAnn, I can kill you and get away with it. After I've done it, I will just sit on the ground, look crazy and keep repeating Saddam Hussain."

Since Roger is a master manipulator, he knew how to turn the tables. I remember his daughter yelling at me on the phone when they asked me to check on him. She told me that he was not okay because he had just come back from getting high. I had moved out for a while due to his increasing use of crack cocaine, and I did not want my granddaughter to keep seeing the madness. His daughter told me I was not the one for him, and that I need to stay away from him. It was her and her husband that asked me to go and check on him. Roger had sent a group text out saying he was going to kill himself. They asked me to call the police so they could do a wellness check. They also asked me to meet the police at the house. I did that, and when Roger came out of the house, he started yelling and telling the police that he does not want me there, and I need to leave.

I was still on the phone with Roger's daughter and her husband. I cannot believe she had the nerve to say this to me. I did not make him smoke crack. He chose to go back to that poison. Yet, Roger's daughter was condemning me because I want to hold him accountable for his actions when he knows what that stuff will do. Her husband called me back and apologized for his wife's actions. He told me that she had blamed her mom for how her father is.

I tried to reach out to some of Roger's family to see how their experience was with Roger and talk to them about his behavior. At first, his older sister would speak to me about Roger's actions and what they went through with him. But after Roger talked to her, in which he gaslighted me, she blocked my phone number, and stop speaking to me.

This incident was the first time Roger left and went back to Houston, and the time he called me a few days later saying that he was going to kill himself. You would think that the things they went through with Roger, they would know that I was not lying on him. It was like I was living in the twilight zone. As if I am this bad and mean person, doing horrible things to Roger, which in my opinion, is why he continues down the road of destruction, and smoking crack. People treat him like he is a child and enable him. I did that for a while, but I grew very tired of it. I was trying to prevent him from being angry at me.

There is one of Roger's sisters that I am thankful for, and she has never stopped speaking to me. She knows her brother, and she was not in denial of what he does. She encouraged me and prayed for us both. She would call and check on me, and we would talk for hours. She would not speak evil about Roger or me. She would just let me vent.

I know you are probably wondering at this point in the book, why would I even marry someone like Roger. I have been wondering the same thing as well.

After so much reflection, self-care, studying the Word for myself, addressing my co-dependency issue, and counseling, I learned that I am incapable of fixing anyone. That is up to God, and I am not Him! I also realized that some of my reactionary behavior shows that I desperately needed areas of improvement within myself. There is no way I should have been yelling back at him. Questioning him about women or even recording him. However, the recording and tracking were from the advice of a police officer.

I realized that I was a battered and abused woman who allowed her husband to continue down the road of degradation without being unchecked to those who needed to know. I did try, but it was too late. I covered up for him so often, just to keep the peace, and so he would not lose his job or go to jail.

I would imagine most abused women are like me, they will try everything to keep their marriage together. Whether it be for the children, financial reasons, or just out of fear of being alone, those are some of the reasons abused women stay with their spouses. We hope things will get better. But, in the end, we know that if our spouse does not seek the help they need, and Roger certainly did not, we know in our hearts that things will not get better. They get worse.

I was not financially dependent on Roger, nor did we have any children together. I sincerely wanted to stay together with Roger because I did not want another failed marriage, and we had started to build something together. Despite his anger, rage, and abuse, I still wanted to worship God together, help him grow Biblically, own a home with him, and go on trips with him, as we often did. Most of the time, at my expense. My fixation on the institution of marriage and I hoped that with prayer, God would heal Roger, and I would be able to stand by his side through anything. Even if it was a false narrative of what our marriage was like in others' eyes, or how we portrayed it to others.

I can remember calling the police out to the house one day, as I had no choice. Roger had just gotten home from a crack binge, and as usual, he would take his anger out on me for failing himself, and more than likely me. I would often threaten Roger by telling him I was going to call the Founder of the organization we worked for if he did not come home. By me doing this, it made Roger more aggressive when he came back home.

Roger loved turning his phone off when he was on a binge, and I would get angry and leave messages on his phone. I would tell him he was a horrible person to just up and go when nothing was wrong. I would try anything to get him to return home. Nothing worked. When Roger wanted to get high on crack, there was nothing that was going to stop him. Not even his wife. I would also try to make him see that he was in a position of prestige and power and that if the Senators and Congressmen knew he had this issue, what would they think. It would bring shame to the Foundation. That did not even work.

The next morning, he would return home, and I knew the whole day would be ruined. Immediately when he came into the house, he would go and find me, wherever I was in the house. He would get in my face, spit in my face, call me bitches and motherfuckers. He would tell me that he did not want me, I was fat, ugly, and I was shaped bad. He would say to me how much he hated me and that I was nothing to him. My response to him most of the time would be, "Roger, I know who I am in Christ Jesus. You can say what you want to about me, but it does not bother me."

Roger saw that the name-calling was not going to get me engaged in a shouting match with him, so he would up the ani. Roger would act as though he was the devil himself, buck his eyes as though he was a madman, tell me I better leave, or else he would do something to me.

He would pull down the attic steps as though he had guns in the attic. Telling me I better go before he kills me, and himself. There was a couple of times where I stood my ground and did not leave. Instead, I went up to our room and took a shower and while in the shower the shower curtains slid back. I looked to see who slid the shower curtains and it was Roger, he had that evil look on his face. In his hand he had the electric heater I was using to keep it warm in the bathroom while I showered. As though as he was going to throw it in the shower to kill me by electrocution. He stared at me for about a minute, more than likely contemplating if he was going to actually do it or not. After his evil stare he closed the shower curtain and left the room.

At this point, I am calling the police because I have had enough of this behavior. When the police arrived, I would tell the officers that he is a veteran who has PTSD, and I just need them to talk to him. I would lie about him threatening me because I did not want them to take him to jail. I would often try to reason with Roger about his anger and rage. Trying to get him to see that he has a prominent position, and he is going to ruin it if he does not get help.

Roger did not care about his position, probably because he knew that he could talk himself out of anything. And pretty much, it worked. He surely has the gift of gab and is good at lying with a straight face. There have been times when I know he is lying, but to keep the peace, I just did not call him on some of the lies he told me.

If he had an important meeting or presentation to go to and missed them, I would lie for him. I would say he was sick or something to cover for him. Although he was in South Atlanta at some motel getting high. It got so bad in the summer of 2018 that an officer from Riverdale, Georgia, called me and said they had Roger in the car. The officer said that someone was concerned about him at the stoplight, and they did not know if he was dead or sleeping. He asked me what was going on.

I told him Roger was a veteran, has PTSD, and has a drug addiction. The officer told me that he usually gives veterans a break for the service of our country. He debated if he was going to take Roger to jail or not. A few minutes later he said, he was going to take Roger to jail, but I am only going to charge him with a misdemeanor.

He told me that I would be able to pick Roger up after a few hours. Roger did not get out of jail until the wee hours of the morning. Roger got upset with me because I did not call around to see if I could bond him out. I was not going to enable him on that occurrence.

After Roger was released, I could tell he was so exhausted and had been on a crack binge for days when he fell asleep at the stoplight in a place he said he did not remember driving. Not to mention he was in a rental when this happened. A few days earlier, Roger was in South Atlanta, where he was exhausted from getting high. So tired that Roger said he was asleep in his truck and it had rolled into a pole, and he had to take it to get the back bumper replaced. He then had damage to the Jeep that was a rental and had to pay the deductible for this, although he has never paid it.

When Roger was jailed for this occurrence, he missed a meeting where I had to cover for him with a lie. His Director from the old organization could not reach him. So, for Roger to keep his position, I lied for him. To this day, his former Director and the men he used to work with and work for now think I am a terrible influence on Roger. They believe I make Roger do the things he does. That I have a spell on him to make him do whatever I say. I literally cannot believe they believe this crap. It is unreal when they know Roger's personality.

I can recall when I first started talking to Roger; he told me that those guys looked up to him, that he could start a cult, and they would believe him. Perhaps this is the reason they believed everything that came out Roger's mouth, is the truth? Roger is so very good at lying and manipulating people. There were times where I would just stare at him lying to someone, in disbelief. Lying does not seem to bother Roger at all; if it does, he does not show it.

The first time I reached out to the Founder of the old Foundation, who is also the Founder of the new organization that I worked for and Roger still does. I reached out to him, crying and told him what was going on. He said I did the right thing, and that he would have someone get Roger back to Camp Hope. A few days later, Roger's Director emailed me and told me to call him; he wanted to talk to me about what I had talked to the Founder about regarding Roger. Instead of me calling, I told Roger about it. Roger went into the garage and got his service dog's leash and threw it across a part of the garage so it could hang as if he were going to hang himself. He started yelling that if he lost his job, he was going to kill himself. I told Roger I was not going to call his Director so that he would calm down. I told him to call Ben, and this is what he did. A few hours later, I was fired from the previous Foundation.

Whatever Roger told them, it got me fired instead of him getting the help he needed. I did not try to defend myself with his Director. Roger threatened me then, telling me that I need to keep our business to ourselves. And it is my fault that I got fired. I could not believe this! How is it that we both work for a foundation that assists veterans with PTSD, which includes addictions, suicidal, etc., and I lose my job by trying to do the right thing. How am I any different from the many wives who use this method to get their husbands some help?

After this, we slowly smoothed things over. Instead of leaving him, I continued to support him with his work for the Foundation.

If he needed a presentation created, I would do it for him. Roger's weekly report, I would do it. Anything he needed so that he would be successful, I did it. He tried to get me hired back on again, but it did not happen. Later in the months, we found out the former Foundation had performed a hostile takeover from the original Founder. The Founder sent an email out to the organization. I told Roger to reach out to the Founder and always keep in contact with him, even if the former Foundation did not want Roger to talk to him. I cared about this man, the Founder. Hearing Roger talking about him in such a great way, I could not help but to love him.

Once the former board members got rid of the Founder, he started another foundation to assist veterans, first responders, and family members with PTSD. It took a while for Roger to work for him because we had done so well with getting veterans to Camp Hope to get the help they needed. I remember the day Roger finally called Mr. Steelwell, the Founder, and told him that he was ready to become the Director of the new Foundation. Mr. Steelwell hired us both the first week in October. We immediately went to work and started reaching out to people to let them know the change. We assembled a team, some from the old Foundation, and some new people.

Mr. Steelwell said he wanted to come to Atlanta to meet the team we had assembled. I immediately went to work with planning it. I made sure everything was professional, made name cards for everyone, was a great host at a downtown hotel conference room. I made sure the food arrived on time. I created a plan for our chapter. Roger gave me two thumbs up and told me he was proud of me. I worked in the corporate world for most of my adult life, plus I have been in the field of project management for over fifteen years. Finally, I thought this was going to work out.

Roger had gone to Arizona to solidify the group there. He stayed with a retired famous race car driver and his wife at their home. I will call the race car driver's wife name, Margie. She introduced Roger to all these famous people to get donations and to support the Foundation. Roger hired her brother to head the chapter in Arizona. He later died from alcohol abuse due to his excessive drinking and PTSD. Roger had fired him probably a month after he relocated to Arizona due to his drinking.

Roger would call me and tell me all the exciting things that were going on in Arizona. At night he would send me a link to Dr. Tony Evans's marriage videos on YouTube so that I could watch them. I just knew that God was changing him. One night I was unable to reach him, so I panicked. I called Margie the next morning, and she told me that his phone had died, and it had messed up. I guess Roger had been talking about me to her because she was under the impression that I was the type to blow his phone up. I did that night because I was afraid that he might have been with another woman. More on this later, as to why I would think that Roger would cheat on me no matter where he is. She said she told him that his good wife, me, would more than likely call to get him a new one. She was right. I called the nearest AT&T store and planned for him to pick up a new phone on my plan. After I had done this, I made sure I sent the address and details to Margie's brother's phone.

Later, Roger told me that Margie had introduced him to this lady who helped other organizations get recognized, and she had all these awards from being a film producer. Roger immediately called Mr. Steelwell about this lady. Mr. Steelwell was smitten by her and quickly brought her on board as the COO. No vetting, no nothing.

Once Roger got back from Arizona, I had already started planning for a Gala Mr. Steelwell wanted to have in 2019.

I set up the conference calls for this with the Founder, Roger, Tim (Executive Director), and the new COO, I will call her Sam. Sam immediately took the lead as to what we wanted to do. I remember her saying that "we can't just simply have a big party and expect it to be a success." I took that as, "this black woman does not know what she is doing."

We planned a meeting with the committee that we had set up for the Gala in December 2018; Sam, Tim, and Mr. Steelwell had scheduled to fly down to be at the Gala committee meeting. I had started the preparation for them to come. One night I was venting to Roger about Sam's attitude when we were getting ready for bed. Roger got so upset with me, put on some clothes, and left. He left the day after Thanksgiving. I called him, no answer, finally, he turned his phone off.

He did not return home until the next day. Of course, I knew this was an opportunity to create an argument to leave and get high. The next day, he had one of the Navy Officer's that works for the Foundation over, and another guy who was in the Army over. He was so belligerent to me in front of them. Roger being hostile with me in front of the company, did not sit well with me, so I mouthed off to him, just as he was doing to me.

While the Navy Officer was visiting, I offered him some gumbo that I had made for Thanksgiving. I warmed him some up in a bowl and went to the neighborhood Dollar Store to get something. Roger asked if I was going to warm him some up as well. I told Roger, "absolutely not" as bad as he talked about me in front of his company, he could get it himself. When I got back from the Dollar Store, I walked in. I got an email notification on my phone; it was from the Executive Director, Tim.

Attached was a letter stating that my employment with the Foundation was terminated. During this time, I was a full-time employee, and they were paying me eight hundred dollars per week before taxes. Because I would not get Roger some gumbo, he called and had me fired.

By Roger doing this, it led to total chaos in our marriage because he had done this to me again. The Army guy who came over that day, less than a year later, called Roger a nigger in his drunken stoop! He was the guy that Roger thought so highly of and would share a marijuana blunt and a six-pack. Roger hired his wife as well, and boy, did she want my position. Once Roger fired me, he got her to take on the responsibilities that I had. It seemed that Roger enjoyed hurting me, and I was the fool for allowing it to continue.

We almost did not recover our marriage at that time, and to be honest, it led me to a state of just surviving and only being in the marriage just for the sake of being in it. Many mornings I would wake up angry. I would be thinking every day to myself; what kind of husband would do this to their wife? Someone who said they would love me, and I could trust. I was wondering if God is seeing what my husband had just done to me. How can he get away with all the lies, deceit, and harsh treatment of me? Now, as I think about it, it is because I allowed it. It had nothing to do with God. I realized that if I let someone mistreat me, I should not expect him to honestly treat me like a husband should treat their wife.

Meanwhile, as the day passed, Roger and I were in a war with one another. He moved out and into a slummy extended stay. Because in his eyes, Roger believed he was right in having me fired. He was right for treating me like a rug you wipe your feet on. But what did I do? I got sucked into his cunning manipulation. He would send me messages of a song we had both listened to often, or kind words. He would call just to say he missed me.

In contrast of what he would have to say about me when he talked to his so-called "mentor," let's call him Bill. He would not have kind words to say about me. Bill has quite the checkered past, and as an Addiction Counselor, you would think that he would have noticed Roger's manipulation. Not Bill. If he did, it is because later he was found out to have been an abuser of "Stolen Valor." As I look back when they first met and why he took a liken to Roger, this is because they are cut from the same demons. He did not care how Roger treated me, so long as Roger forgave him for "Stolen Valor." Roger often told me about Bill and his unsavory ways.

The illegal ammunition in his home is enough to start a war. The "ears" that were supposed to be from his days in special forces. Supposedly Bill was taken prisoner in a camp in Vietnam. His captures allegedly cut open his stomach and left his organs hanging. Yet he escaped, cut their throats, and saved the ears he cut off as a trophy. That is what he told Roger anyway. We later learned that none of it was true. Once the heat was on Bill's deception, he needed Roger to come over to his home and remove all the guns and other devices from his home. Roger did not hesitate to go and oblige his so-called mentor. He told me how he took something like one of those military machine guns to a lake and threw it as far as he could. The other weapons and artillery he took to one of his employee's homes. Every time Bill needed something for Roger to do, Roger would be like a slave. Making sure he met every request, Bill asked of him.

Meeting Bill's every request also drove a wedge in our marriage. So often, Roger would meet the demands of everyone else, everyone except me, his wife. I came last to everything and everyone.

We often gave a false narrative in front of most of our family. Also, to people, Roger wanted to buy into the Foundation.

After, even him firing me again, I remained faithful to the cause. Still, I would prepare his material for meetings or events. Making sure he had everything he needed to be successful. Roger would use reverse psychology on me. He would say, "if you do not do it, I will just get so and so to do it."

Let's go back a bit. I want to talk about the retired famous racecar driver's wife for a bit. I call her Margie. She is someone that has major skills when it comes to scoring money. When she found out that Roger no longer worked for the previous foundation, she reached out to him and said she was sticking with Roger and the current foundation. Of course, she knew Mr. Steelwell had money.

Margie had already been in the Arizona newspapers on the news due to her previous employees and son accusing her of racism and a hostile work environment. Roger later admitted to me that the only reason Margie contacted him and pretended to be his friend is that she knew he would be a gateway to Steelwell. And was he right.

Roger could not resist women praising him for his work. Especially women who were somewhat "famous". I got to go to Arizona with Roger in 2019 to attend the St. Jude's Gala, we were Margie's guest. She also made sure Steelwell would come as well. I do not believe she wanted me to come, as she stated it in one of her conversations to Roger, she asked if I was going to come. I say that because of the way she asked Roger the question.

Margie had been confiding in Roger about losing the race car driving school, and the creditors she owed. She had put her husband in a facility, so she was strapped for cash. I also know this, because she asked Roger if he thought Steelwell would loan her a half million dollars. Stay with me as I believe I pointed out systemic racism in previous pages. Here we are again. When we made it to Arizona, Roger did not have a dime. I had gotten a loan for our airline tickets. He was too coward to ask Steelwell to pay for them.

I rented the car with my credit card and paid for all our meals. When we went shopping, I paid for everything. While we were there, Margie asked me if I would help her get logged back on to one of her bank accounts. I helped her do it. I am not sure why, but from what I saw she was broke, but she also wanted me to help her set up the bill pay feature from that account. After seeing some of the things I saw, I had a talk with Roger about it afterward.

I knew Steelwell was thinking about loaning her the money, or he had told Margie he would loan it to her. So, after talking with Roger he called Steelwell and had me tell Steelwell what I saw. I expressed to Steelwell that if it were me, and seeing that the numbers did not add up, he would be giving Margie a half million dollars. She could not pay him back. He said he was not going to do it, initially. But, apparently, she got Roger and him back out to Arizona one more time alone, and Steelwell came off the half million dollars.

Margie would set up these fruitless meetings with people who supposedly had some interest in the organization. Either some of the people were a no show, or nothing came from the meeting.

The last time I talked to Roger back in April 2020, he communicated to me that Margie had not paid Steelwell back, and she told Steelwell that he had said on many occasions that his money is the Lord's money and not his. We all know what that means. LOL! Margie had agreed to pay Steelwell back once the home in Paradise Valley Arizona sold. The home has since been auctioned off, and as of May 2020 it is owned by Jacob and Nicea Walker Family Trust, which is a Silverstrand Fund I, LLC company. It is funny, but not. I recall telling Roger that Margie's home will not sell due to putting away her husband in the manner in which she did. I can recall being there and we had gone to get lunch.

We stopped by the facility where Margie's husband resided to bring him along. As we were leaving the restaurant, I recall Mr. "Vonder" asking Margie, when will he be coming home. He gave her a kiss that she was not apparently expecting. She wiped his kiss from her lips and whispered to herself, "Honey, you are not coming back home." Well, maybe she thought no one was going to hear her, but I certainly did. There were a couple of times when I could not go in the facility and sit with them. I stood outside and cried, because I knew this was a place where this man did not want to be.

When we got back to Margie's home, I told Roger about it. He brushed it off since it was coming from me. Roger always thought I was bitter, or not giving the women the benefit of the doubt, he brought into the organization from Arizona. Margie had such influence on Steelwell that she got her daughter involved with the organization.

One day we were on a conference call planning for the Gala we had back in 2019. Margie's daughter was on the call as well. Steelwell asked me to make phone calls to corporate leaders and the professional sports teams, to set appointments for donations and sponsorships for the Gala. What he said next was an insult to me. After he told me to make the appointments, he said he was going to fly Margie's beautiful daughter out to meet with the people for the appointments I set. I thought wow, "What am I? Ugly or something? Not the right color to be beautiful? Does he not believe I know how to have a dialog with professionals at the C-level?" It was pointless to bring it up to Roger, to share my feelings about Steelwell's statement. Bettye was not allowed to express her feelings, only Roger was allowed to do that.

I had tried to reach out to Margie a few times regarding Roger's abuse. A few times I talked to her and she told me she was going to talk to Steelwell about it. Whether she did or not, I cannot say. I do know she did get to see a glimpse of Roger's rage when we were in Arizona in April 2019.

Roger was very strategic. He would often tell me that I would never beat him at this game. He said he learned from his military experience, so there was no way I could beat him. What Roger never learned, when married, there are no games. We should have been on the same team. He was right in the fact that no one was going to believe me, and no one would be on my side. To be honest. I was hurt by this fact. People feared Roger. I do not know why, but they did. No one crossed him when it came to him vs. me. There are people on my Facebook page to this day, who are mutual friends with Roger, and they fear to even "like" or "comment" on a post I make. They will look though, but that is about it. There is a reason I have not blocked them all, and when the time comes, they will understand why I have yet to block them.

You would think the numerous times where I have been played on many occasions, I would have learned my lesson, but there would be many times I would be by Roger's side during some of his meetings and events, pretending to be happy. Swallowing my pride and walking in humility. It is funny how, in most of Roger's speeches, he would say, "he is just helping his brothers find their way out of the darkness, as someone helped him do. Every time he said this, I would say to myself, "this is such a lie. You have not found your way out of the darkness. You are still in darkness." After all, he would have just gotten home that morning from being on a crack binge the night before.

There were times when I did see a glimmer of hope. I thought God was finally answering my prayers. Give Roger a renewed heart, sound mind, a new spirit of humility, kindness, patience, and love. We started going to church at St. James United Methodist Church in Alpharetta, Georgia.

It felt good, and I thought, finally, we have found a place where we are going to grow spiritually together. We even attended this eight-weeks class together, which we thought brought us closer together. Except towards the end, Roger fell back and decided he needed to get high. I pressed through, even though Roger did not arrive with me. He showed up towards the latter part of the class. I remember sending an email that morning, asking our class to pray for him. When he walked in, I was happy to see he pressed through his demons. But going home was a different dilemma. He reminded me of the voicemail messages I left on his phone, telling him he was satan's spawn, and he did not have God in him.

I must admit that I left some offensive messages on his phone when he pulled one of his moves to get high. He called me so many bitches, motherfuckers that it was almost normal to me. I am sure that his outburst of anger and rage was normal to our neighbors as well. I would head for the door when he came back home from being on a crack binge.

The guy across the streets came out one day and told Roger to shut up. Why was Roger upset with the neighbor, when it was him disturbing the peace in the neighborhood? Roger replied in a rage, "fuck you, fuck you motherfucker". I knew the routine. He would storm through the door and say, "you talk that shit now that you left on my phone.

You ugly fat bitch!" He would often say that nobody wanted me, that I was built funny, unattractive, and talked about my body parts. Any horrible thing you can think of to make someone feel insecure, he said it to me. And after a day or so, Roger gives me his depression talk and thinks homicidal, wanting to go kill up a bunch of people. He would tell me that he knows he does not like saying those horrible things to me. That he wants to kill himself, and he is so depressed that he does not want to get off the couch. There were times where he would stay on the sofa without taking a bath or eating anything.

He would just look at his phone a bit, ignore phone calls, and stare into space. What do I do? I felt terrible by my actions, as I got sucked into his manipulation every time. Not thinking that I did nothing to make him go out and get high, I blamed my reaction to his actions. I would pray for him and ask God to help Roger with his addiction. To help us in our marriage and to humble me and not react negatively, even if Roger instigated an argument so that he could leave. Each time I failed! One reason is that we would be laughing in the middle of the day, having a great time.

We would have just made love, and not even four hours would have past, where there would be something wrong where Roger needed to go and get high. I would say to him, "What is up with you? Did we not just make love, and now you are leaving"? I felt like a cheap prostitute at times, and I told him this.

It did not matter how good a wife I was to Roger; I would have dinner prepared and ask him if he needed something, yet it was still not enough. I would buy him expensive colognes, or a nice shirt I saw at Dillard's or Nordstrom's, the happiness, often short-lived. The pain I felt each time Roger would yell at me was like a knife piercing my stomach. Very painful to see him act the way he often did and talk the way he often talked.

Yet, in all of this, I was too embarrassed to say anything to the people that mattered. When attending support groups for spouses every week, I did not share many things in our support groups because I did not want Roger's reputation tarnished. I would listen to the other women share their pain, but I would share very little with them as though our marriage was on track, and we had truly overcome the darkness that comes with PTSD. I mean, we were the leaders of the organization, so we had to keep the visage of a power couple who are going to impact the community we served.

The Other Women

Roger had insisted that his love was only for me. And that he has graduated from even wanting to be with another woman. He assured me being with another woman was something he had no interest. That he had enough sex in his lifetime with other women, and sex was not something he would even consider being that his marriage was the most important thing to him.

He insisted that I have often accused him of being with other women, which I have a couple of times. His definition of my accusing him of being with other women is me asking him about a few other women contacting him. In his eyes, even if I asked about a woman, I am accusing him. I would ask him about other women, and if you bear with me, you will see that I was well within my rights as a wife.

When Roger first left for Houston when we lived in Rockwall, Texas, he contacted his ex-girlfriend to get him a cellphone. I had looked at our cell phone records,' and I noticed he had called her several times, so when he contacted me, I asked him why was he talking to his ex. His excuse was he needed a cell phone, and she tried to get him one, but she was not able to. I asked him if it would be okay if I contacted my ex if I needed something because I was upset with him. He could not answer that question, and I am more than sure that he would not have been okay with it. I can remember not too long ago; he told me that if I were ever with another man and if he found out about it, he would kill us both.

Roger loved to bring up old stuff when he would come back home after being on a crack binge. He would often say, "You accused me of being with your sister." I am sure you are wondering if this is true. My answer is yes, it is true. I noticed Roger would always text one of my sisters in the morning with a "good morning" text. I asked him why just this one sister when I have four other sisters. He responded that I was the one that gave me her number. He had two of my other sisters' numbers as well.

When we first moved to Georgia, we were at my sister's home, and we were getting ready to go to our hotel. Out of the blue, Roger played this song to my sister, "Will You Keep Me in Mind." Now me knowing that every song Roger has played for me had a meaning behind it. I asked him, why did he play that song for her. He got upset and told me that he would not even speak to my sister again. I learned that some things are not worth mentioning. However, my discernment would not allow me to keep quiet.

In December of 2018, when I was terminated from the Foundation, again. Roger enlisted my sister to help with duties for the Foundation. He says that another lady who works for the Foundation ordered my sister business cards and the facilitator course and, and he only asked her to help with the Gala. I asked Roger why did he do this? I knew why he did it to hurt me. Roger knew what buttons to push, and he knew what would hurt me. I can recall coming from downstairs one evening. Roger was on the phone with my sister and telling her about our argument. He did not tell her he had been on yet another crack binge. They laughed at me as if I were a child in how kids make fun of another for childish things. I could not believe that my sister would play a role in Roger's evil deeds. But later I realized, she was a victim as well.

Later in December, Roger had left home, and my sister had left her home as well. I know this because we had all put Life360 on our phones to keep track of one another, except for Roger. I saw that they both were nearby, and I assumed they were going to be together. I left a message on Roger's phone telling him I see they are together. He immediately called my sister and told her what I said. She took me off her circle on Life360, and she also blocked me on Facebook. It took a while for my sister and me to talk again. When I would go with Roger at his request to sit in on a group, my sister would be there, and she would not even say anything to me. As if I was a ghost or something. Roger knew how to isolate me from my family.

He would get upset with me if I wanted to go and visit them. He would often say, "your family does not love you". Or, he would bring up our disagreements and things that I shared with him in confidence. Roger's plan was always to divide and conquer. To cause division when he felt as though he might be left alone.

Another woman that I would like to mention is one that popped up again during our first few months in the home we rented in Cumming Georgia. Roger must have forgotten that when we first started talking, he told me about many of his ex-girlfriends. This one rang his cell phone one evening out of the blue. I asked him who was he talking to, as he seemed so happy to hear from her. He told me her name, which I will not mention. That she was a childhood friend, and his sisters know her and grew up with her. I started thinking to myself. Nah, this is not a childhood friend. I knew it was the lady he used to live within Houston; this is what I was saying to myself. He went in the backyard, and although he had her on speakerphone so I could hear, he believed this would ease my mind — silly me.

I allowed them to talk and did not make a fuss of it. But it was heavy on my mind. She would call often, and one day I said to Roger, "She is not a childhood friend, do not you remember telling me about you and her lived together, she left you and moved back to Arkansas"? He kept denying it. But the detective in me would not let it rest. So, I reached out to my oldest sister and one of my cousin's and asked them about this person. They confirmed what I had been thinking all along. I was furious at her and Roger. Why would he lie to me about this? Realizing this is not a man that loves or respects his wife. He still tried to deny it, and finally came clean.

Yet and still, their conversations did not end with him coming clean. We went to Arkansas for the fourth of July in 2018. Roger wanted to go fishing the next morning; we arrived in Arkansas. He left the hotel around 6:00 AM on his way to go fishing alone. Several hours past, I had gotten dressed to visit with our relatives. Roger comes to pick me up from the hotel, and we head to my oldest daughter's home to bring the fireworks we had brought for the grandchildren. I was sitting in the truck with two of my granddaughters listening to music. Roger was outside the truck with my grandson and showing him, the various types of fireworks we had bought. Roger's phone rings on the Bluetooth in the truck. I said to him, "It is so and so". He says to me, "Answer it". I answer it, and it is her. She says, "Hey, you called? I was calling you back". Roger goes on to say that, yes, he called her as he wanted her to meet me. I immediately say out loud, "I do not want to meet your ex-girlfriend". He played it off and told me to hang up the phone. He then got upset and told me to get out of the truck. He peeled off from my daughter's home, cussing and talking loud like some deranged lunatic. I had to get a ride from someone else to go back to the hotel. I was livid!

How are you going to get mad at me because of the wrong you are doing? This woman felt so comfortable that she asked Roger to send her some money. I was amazed that he told me this. Yet he had the nerve to ask me if it was okay for him to send her some. Are you serious?! You would ask me this question!

It was his birthday, Roger was in the bathroom, and this text came through from this same ex-girlfriend from Arkansas, wishing him a happy birthday. I called her and told her that if she contacted him again, I would be making a call to her boyfriend and let him know that she had talked to my husband. I got no reply, and after that, Roger blocked her number. Of course, it was more than likely to appease me.

Shall we go on to the next one?! Let's shall! I assume Roger met this woman in Atlanta being on one of his crack binges. Since she is a mutual friend on Facebook with one of the veteran's he picked up at the Atlanta airport. The guy with a history of a crack cocaine addiction, and the first day all this madness started to begin. After Roger picked him up and did not return home until the next morning. I am not assuming, Roger admitted it to me that he "slipped".

One morning as we started our routine. Starbucks coffee, on the hill to meditate, listen to the gospel, and pray. Roger stopped at the Dollar Store to get cigarettes. He left his phone in the truck. This picture comes across his screen, and I look at it. I wonder, who is this woman sending a photo with a lightning bolt and a set of red lips? Not again?! Roger gets back in the truck, and he always could tell when something was not settling in my spirit. He asked, "What's wrong with you"? I asked him about the picture, and Roger looks at it. He says, "That's Jarvis. She's not wrapped to tight". He goes on to tell me that she is married. He knew I was not buying it, so he asked me if I wanted him to call her. I told him yes, call her. Roger calls her, and she answers the phone. He goes on to say that he was with me and I could hear her, and I wanted to know why she was sending him a picture of her.

I guess Roger was not expecting the response she gave. Jarvis says, "I sent you this picture because I was thinking about you. The lightning bolt represents how you make me feel when I am with you, and the kiss was me sending you a good morning kiss. I also sent you a song by SWV, I Get Weak in the Knees". None of her truths phased Roger; he played it off and told her to put some guy on the phone he knew there. I know what you all must be saying, and trust me, I have said it to myself repeatedly, "I was a damn fool"! I concur!

To this day, Roger still says nothing happened with him and Jarvis. We all know this is a lie! She tried to resurface about ten months ago as we were on our way to get coffee and do our morning routine. We were headed to Starbucks that morning. Roger's phone ring from a number that was not saved in his phone. He answered it. The voice said, "Hello Roger, good morning". He asked, "Who is this"? When she told him it was Jarvis, he told her do not ever call his phone again, and he hung up the phone. After he did that, he said, "Wow, look at the devil"! We were having these same issues, but we were trying to get back on track. When the enemy knows there are issues in any relationship or marriage, it is his opportunity to devour and destroy.

Oh, the ex-wife that lives in the Little Rock, Arkansas area. The second time I was terminated from the Foundation. I had gotten Roger's old phone repaired. It needed a battery. I opened his Facebook page and learned that he and his ex-wife had been talking on the phone. After things died down and we reconciled, I asked him why was he talking to his ex-wife? Again, he made the excuse that he needed to talk to somebody. I am confident that I could not have used this excuse. Had I attempted to conversate with my ex anything, I probably would have been picking up my teeth off the floor? Or, had a busted lip before I could explain that he gave?

Lina, baby momma drama. This lady must have been stalking Roger's page. The minute we first went to Arkansas together during our first Christmas alone, she sent me this long message about how Roger abused her. Hindsight, I wished I would have listened to her.

When Roger told his older sister about what Lina had sent to me, his sister denied any of this. Lina would send me messages ever so often, to try and get me to leave Roger. I would show the texts to Roger, and he would shake his head and tell me to block her.

Lina would always send messages through her and Roger's daughter's Facebook page. There were times when she would send subtle messages to Roger, asking him for money and other stuff. Lina started doing this because she saw how well Roger was doing and how we seemed happy together. So, she thought! Roger wanted to see his daughter, and I wanted him to see her as well. Yet, he has told people that I am the reason he did not have a relationship with his daughter, which is, again, such a freakin lie!

I often reached out to Amanda on behalf of Roger to get her to see her dad, and I have the text messages to prove it. I would even send her money via MoneyGram for Roger. I stopped doing it because he did not seem to care, although he told her that he would start sending her $100.00 per week now that she was eighteen and getting ready to start college. The times that I would reach out to her to see if Roger could see her, she would say she would think about it, or she would talk to her mom. Roger even asked me to tell her about the free money available to her since he was a disabled veteran.

Amanda did not seem interested in taking anything from Roger. I cannot say I blame her. If Roger did all to her that Lina said she did, and Roger admitted to me that he had talked to her while Steelwell was in the truck with him when they had the initial meeting planning for the Gala. Roger said he remembered as she spoke to him about the horrible things' he had done to her. This explains why, after we had reconciled, Steelwell called Roger when we were taking a road trip for our second wedding anniversary. He was not aware that Roger and I had reconciled, so he called Roger a sly dog. He said to Roger that Roger was keeping a secret. He thought Roger was with another woman and seemed to be happy about it. I could not believe what I was hearing. He was condoning Roger cheating.

How could someone who profess to be a Christian, and married, condone another married man cheating? It is beyond my comprehension! Roger got upset about this. We were almost in Little Rock, going to visit his son and daughter in law. He started going over ninety miles per hour. I had to tell him to slow down. Roger often did this when he got upset. Drove erratic, or extremely fast, he knew it scared me. There would be times where he would press on the brakes so hard on the interstate, just to rattle me.

If Roger and Lina spoke, he would not do it around me. There were times when he would talk to her around me when he was trying to be kind to me. But not when he was upset with me. He had told me that he believed Lina was using Amanda's Facebook page or phone to text him and ask him for money. She even asked him to get a house in his name for her.

I recently talked to Lina, and she told me the times she would speak with Roger. She recalls talking to him when he would be in his truck in our driveway. She communicated to me that I would come out of the house, and he would say to her on the phone, "Here this bitch comes. I cannot stand her ass".

She also told me that when her and Roger were together, he said he would never be with a black woman, that he could not stand black women. I laughed about that because he does the same thing when he is with a black woman.

This last woman that I know of is a doozy! It is the ultimate betrayal and the occurrence that ended our marriage. Karmai Alexander is a woman that came into Roger's life when we first started working with the previous Foundation, if not three years ago, almost three years ago. I do not know if she had seen a post on Facebook from Roger, or she contacted the corporate office, and they gave her Roger's number since his number was listed for the Georgia chapter. Karmai reached out to him and asked him if the Foundation had any assistance for women veterans. They talked on the phone for a while. He told her we did not and referred her to some other well-known organizations.

They became friends on Facebook, and Roger would let me see some of Karmai's artistry work. He would comment that she has some significant issues, but she does great artwork. I agreed that her artwork was pretty good.

We were looking for people to donate auction items for the Gala we had in October of 2019 at the Fox Theatre. Roger asked me if he should ask Karmai to do a piece for us. I did not have any problem with it and thought it would be a great idea. Perhaps she would get some more exposure for her work. Karmai agreed to do a piece, and when the time came for Roger to pick the piece up, he told me he was going to meet her in Atlanta. We invited Karmai to the Gala. However, she later told Roger that she did not have the gas money for parking. When Roger picked the piece up, he and Karmai took a picture, and she tagged him on the photo. I saw it, and I thought, "There is something about that pose that does not sit well with my spirit." I ignored it and commented that her work was awesome, and I "loved" the photo.

She painted an eagle on a coffee table for us. Roger brought it home, and he commented that she did a second-rate job because the laminate on it had split. I told him that was no big deal, and it looked good. I start noticing how Roger would make sure his phone was turned face down. And instead of entering a password to unlock it, he used his fingerprint to unlock his phone. I did not say anything, but I did notice it. We all know that when someone is up to no good, they will put their phone on silent, vibrate, lock their phone, or turn it face down. With Roger, he made sure I could not access his cell phone.

In addition to him acting more dramatic and irritated at anything, I would ask him. Even if it were asking him, "Would you like to go get some coffee"? He would say "no" in a harsh voice. As if I was getting on his nerves. The writing was on the wall. I just did not know who she was. That is, not until I got fired for the third time at the end of 2019.

Roger had not blocked me on Facebook, although he had moved out. I would read his post, and I noticed Karmai would comment on Roger's post with a heart, praying hands, and an emoji with hearts all over it. Again, I probably should have been a private detective. I went to her page, and I noticed she had started posting the "No One Heals Alone" tag line. It is the Steelwell's Foundation's tag line.

I then saw a picture she had posted with Roger, another guy that works for the foundation, her, and another woman. Say it ain't so?!

Yes, so! Roger had replaced me with Karmai Alexander. Yes, you heard me, right! He had me fired, and I will explain that in more detail, only to have her hired so that he would still be able to have more income after he left me. I was very hurt when I saw this. I cannot even explain the hurt I felt. The betrayal I felt!

To make matters worse, he even took a picture of her standing by the truck I co-signed for with Zapp, Roger's service dog. And the dog that would protect me from his rage.

Roger knew I love Zapp, but here we are again, a man who will hurt people without a conscience, and as if he is working for the devil. Inflict as much pain on me, and without any regard of us still being married.

All I could think about was the moral, financial, and administrative support I gave this man to uplift his image and success in his position. The thousands of dollars and hours I spent on clothes, suits, shoes, watches, cologne, business trips, built up his credit, creating his presentations, picking up printing materials, saving the foundation thousands of dollars, and, etc. Just so he could arrive and get to where he needed to be, toss me away like I was trash. Not only Roger but Steelwell as well.

When Steelwell paid tens of thousands of dollars for a brochure, and a crappy website as Roger and all agreed for the veterans and first responders, it was a waste of money. I helped revise it for the better. The website was horrible. I worked with the web developer and wrote the content for the new website. I was not paid anything extra. When a lady referred by Margie to write a press release for us, Steelwell did not like it. I rewrote it, and he loved it. I got everything prepared to have it released by NPR but received nothing extra as far as compensation.

When I noticed the invoices were overbilled after the Gala, I brought it to Steelwell's attention, and he asked me to itemize and create a spreadsheet for each line item, I did that. I saved them over ten thousand dollars. I got nothing extra. The only thing I received was being fired. And another woman had taken my husband and given a position with the foundation from Roger's referral.

I can recall one day after I had tried to reach out to Steelwell and Bill for intervention.

Again, Roger made sure he poisoned me good this time. He called Steelwell on the phone, put the call on the speaker, and the conversation went like this.

Roger: "Mr. Steelwell, I have you on speaker, and BettyeAnn is listening. Didn't you say if BettyeAnn reached out to you or anyone else about me, she would be fired"? Steelwell: "Yes." End of conversation. My heart sunk into my stomach. I knew that by Steelwell saying this, it gave Roger reign to do anything and treat me anyway without any accountability or repercussion. And man, was I right, after this, Roger told me that Steelwell had given him money to hire an attorney for the divorce.

The day I left in November to go to Virginia to assist one of the volunteers with outreach, support groups, and solicit some donors for the organization, Roger was in an uproar.

The morning I was getting ready to go and get the rental car, Roger kept calling me bitches, motherfuckers, he even got Bill on the phone while doing all of this. He told me my car had better not be in the way or else he was going to have it towed. I just know that Roger had not slept here the night before. I was trying to be kind to him before I left, but he made sure that he was not kind to me. Before I left, I made sure my car was not blocking the garage. It was like I was living in the twilight zone!

I did not know where all this rage and anger were coming from with Roger. Perhaps he had lied on me so much to Steelwell and Bill that they may have told him to get away from me, and maybe he regretted lying on me because now he had to act.

I kept praying for Roger and asking God to help him. I guess God was saying to me that if I have not gotten the message by now of the type of man I am dealing with, I will never get it. It is not up to me to change Roger, Roger must want to change, and only he can seek God if that is what he wants.

A couple of nights before I was to head back to Georgia, Roger called me multiple times. A few times, he talked as though we were going to make it work.

Two nights before I left to head back to Georgia, Roger called upset, saying that he was at the house because he thought I was going to be there, and he wanted to see me. He took photos of the house to let me know I was not there in the rental. I told him he was mistaken, and I do not know where he got the idea that I would be home that night. As I headed back home, I got a call from Steelwell, and I texted him that I was driving and could not text him back. He then called me to see how the trip went.

I gave him the run-down of our daily activities, as it seemed that he was pleased once we hung up the phone. As you can see, although the trip was a success, it did not matter; I was fired a week after. Roger called me when I was almost home, to let me know he had moved out, but he was willing to do anything to make our marriage work. He went on to say he is ready to go to counseling at the church I had just started going to, he was willing to go to church with me on Sunday, and Wednesday evening Bible study. I do not know if Roger and Karmai had been talking or not, since Roger communicated to me what his plans were. I would not have expected they were, since he was willing to do all of this; of course, I was wrong. Roger even came over one evening and brought over wine, candles, slippers for him and me.

He brought white t-shirts for us to wear that night. He went upstairs and ran bath water for me to take a bath so that he could rub me down with baby oil and give me a massage. That night was something I believe we both wanted. He stayed the night, the next morning we went in separate cars to go and eat breakfast. After that, we went to his extended stay room. When we got there, his phone went off, he looked at it and said oh, that's just Karmai asking me a question. I did not think anything of it at the time.

He had told me that he was only ten minutes away from me and that if I needed him, call. And that was about right. He also told me that he would help me pay the rent, but I better not say anything to anybody. I thought that was weird for him to say that. Why would he care if he wants to help his wife? I am assuming he did not want Bill or Steelwell to know that he was willing to help me.

Roger had mentioned to me that he had called the electric company to let them know we were moving, and they were going to turn the lights off.
So, I called them and told them we changed our minds and not to shut the lights off.

The next day Roger came over with coffee in his hands for him and I. I was upstairs, and he was downstairs, and I could hear him talking to the lady at the utility company to let them know we were not moving. He seemed surprised to hear from the representative at the utility company that I had already called. I could hear him say, "Oh, she did." Once he got off the phone, he seemed upset because I had done what he asked me to do. Roger had not moved the rest of his clothes and items out of the house. But, after the phone call, he became in a rage and started moving his things in his truck.

Before I knew it, he started talking about the tracker I left in his truck. The more he thought about my reactions in the past to his actions; he became more enraged. I left because he turned in to a different person. It scared me because he went to the gas stove, turned on the gas under each eye so the house could fill up with gas. His words were, "Bitch, you are going to die today." He blamed me for the way our marriage was and that I was not going to ruin his career. I would make a circle back to the house to see if he had gotten all his things, but he was still in the home. I came back in after a while because I was tired of just driving.

He then brought up that I needed to give him the $200.00 he put in my account a month or so ago before this event. I told him I did not have $200.00 and that we are married. I told him as many times as I have given him money, and my bank card so that he could have money was not something I wanted back, because a married couple should have each other's back.

He did not want to hear that. He took my cell phone, and he saw my laptop bag that had my laptop and iPad in it and said he was going to take that if I did not give him the $200.00. He started running off with it, and I ran to the neighbors to use their phone to call the police. My neighbor answered the door, but he knew what was going on. He came out to try and talk to Roger. Roger as always, relives old things that were irrelevant to what was currently taking place, and went in about the tracker I placed on the truck. He then allowed the neighbor to listen to my voicemails that I had left on his cell phone when he would be on his crack binges. I left without calling the police. Once Roger saw my neighbor, he brought my cell phone and laptop bag to me.

After this episode, I only saw Roger once. Of course, there was an evening when he called me in a panic. About a week later, Roger called me to tell me he did not trust anyone. He was at the house and wanted to see me. I told him I was over to one of my sisters about five minutes away and that I would meet him there. Once I pulled up, Roger sped out of the driveway. He saw a car parked by our curb. I called Roger and asked what was going on with him? And why did he leave like that? He said he thought I was up to something, and he felt it was my sister's vehicle. He knew that it was not my sister's vehicle. That car that was on the curb was white, and my sister's vehicle is black. I told him this, and he never came back.

One last effort. I emailed Roger and told him I had made an appointment for Roger and me to see the Associate Pastor at the church I had just started attending. He agreed to meet me there. It was a muted point. Roger could only talk about old things that I had said or accused him of what happened over two years ago. He brought up the tracker.

The Associate Pastor asked him if he could not see why I would ask him about other women, being that he often entertained his ex-girlfriends. He said that he could see that. Roger communication switched so that of someone who is not familiar with an event that supposedly happened to him, they would feel sorry for him. He talked about his best friend dying in his arms. Before he could get it out, I said, "Oh, boy." That made Roger upset, and this is the last time I have seen Roger. He got up and walked out of the session. Roger would often talk to me about this after he got in his depressed mood after he has realized that he had just spent a boatload of money on crack. He would cry and talk about how people do not understand what he has gone through. The stress of the work he is doing with other veterans and listening to them on a constant.

Perhaps it sounds like I am a heartless person. Quite the contrary. It is just that I have listened to these excuses over, and over again. Roger has always made himself to be the victim. I would often tell him that Christ has set us free. That whatever we have done in our past, or experienced by others, if we do not learn to forgive, we will never be able to move forward to a bright future. It only seemed to register in Roger's mind for a short time when he needed me.

I kept thinking about Karmai and Roger. I had seen on Facebook, where she had started to be friends with people in our circle. I saw a picture she had posted with Roger and the guys in the support groups.

I had to know for sure and see for myself, so I rented an SUV to get close and personal. Yes, it sounds crazy, and I admit it was a bit off the chart.

I waited until the evening on that Thursday to go to the parking lot where I knew the support group were being held. I waited there for almost three hours. I would see Roger come in and out of the group to smoke a cigarette; he would be talking to some of the women outside smoking. I saw this man who kept going to the passenger side of the truck, opening the door and talking to Roger. Mind you; this is the truck I co-signed for him.

After a while, I saw Karmai get out of the passenger side to go into Ingles. I mean, I saw this, but it is something I was hoping that I was making this all up in my head. It was not! My adrenaline was so high, that I became overwhelmingly nervous. I am so glad I did not have a gun that night. There is no telling what I would have done to them both.

When they pulled off, I started to follow them. I mean, my adrenaline was on one thousand! I guess Roger noticed someone following him, so he quickly pulled off the road. I called him and went off on him. How dare he tell me that I am accusing him of other women when he has one in our truck. Now I am putting this all together in my head.

Usually, if Roger and I argue, or even if I stay in a hotel while he cools off. He would often call me. It was not the case after he started talking to Karmai. She is smooth; I must give her that. And here is why I say, "she is smooth."

I contacted this older man from Massachusetts. I saw him in anguish about something that had to do with Karmai from one of the Facebook pages I was still an editor for, for the foundation. So, I contacted him on Facebook and asked him to call me. Once he called me, he told me that he had been in the hospital under suicide watch. He said to me how Karmai had made it seemed like she loved and cared for him.

He had been taking care of Karmai since 2017. He was a widow and was lonely. Karmai saw this and more than likely thought, "I have found a fool." He told me how he had sent her all this money since 2017 and flowers every month. Once she started seeing my husband, she broke off all communication with him. He said the last time he talked to her was the first part of December, as she told him she needed to buy Christmas gifts after he sent the money, blocked him on Facebook, his phone number and deleted any interaction he had with her on Facebook. He said the heartache almost cost him his life. This man is seventy-seven years of age. I do not know how old Karmai is, but I know she is more than likely ten years or more, younger than Roger and I are.

Mr. Engels had filed charges against Karmai for Larceny and Fraud. I do not believe he followed through, and perhaps had a change of heart. There are laws for taking advantage of and preying on elderly people. Mr. Engels seems to be an intelligent man who trusted his heart to a predator.

He communicated to me that he had kept every text message, every MoneyGram receipt, Western Union receipt, and every document of all the financial assistance he has provided to her. Even the naked photos she sent to him. He said she moved so many times, and the last time he sent money to her, she had given him an address to a parking lot. He told me that he even reached out to Roger and talked to him about what Karmai had done, but Mr. Engels said Roger did not seem as though he cared. I said to him; Roger does not care.

Mr. Engels also said that he tried to talk to one of the employees of the foundation who Roger is now staying. He said this gentleman told him he did not want to hear it and do not call him with that mess. He is the same man that I reached out to, who Roger now lives. He told me the same thing and for me not to ever contact him again.

I was like, "WOW"! The same guy whom I would do his weekly reports for, and without hesitation. The guy that would ask me to revise documents for him and make flyers for him. The guy that I told Roger to make sure he would get some exposure when Roger would go on speaking events. The guy that I advocated for, when Roger was going to give the Georgia Director position to another man who was only sitting at home getting drunk every day and flirting with other women. The guy I stressed to Roger and the foundation, let us call him Cary, he worked more hours than anyone and deserved to be paid full-time pay, instead of part-time pay.

I remember we had a conference call before the Gala to elect Cary and Dr. Boston to receive an award for all the hard work they were doing for veterans. That idea was knocked down. Dr. Boston and some of his advocators, including Cary, wanted to know if some of the funds brought in from the Gala would go to Dr. Boston. Roger got upset and said that everybody wants money and does not want to do anything. Other than have their hands out.

I tried to explain to Steelwell, Roger, and the other people who were on the conference call that Dr. Boston does a lot of work in the community with no pay, and it would seem to me that since this is the largest group in the entire foundation, it would make sense. Cary even asked me if I would create a letter to handout at the groups for those seeking Dr. Boston's assistance with their claims. It was a letter to ask them to consider donating a small amount or percentage of their benefits to Dr. Boston so that he would be able to continue his work for the veterans that need his service. I was honored to do it, and I did it with expediency.

I am amazed at the depths of Roger's manipulation, lies, and deceit to people who believed he is the victim, and I was this horrible mean wife, taking advantage of a disabled veteran.

I have learned from a few folks; I was taking advantage of Roger and his disability. Cary even told someone we both have a connection with, that I am not what they think I am. I had a mutual friend of Roger and me, tell me that Roger needs grace and that he needs love. She also said to me, "How do you know Roger is smoking crack? How do you know that he is not flipping his money?" This more than likely something Roger said to her. When I told her that I have been intimate with Roger, but each time I do, he makes me feel like a prostitute. She understood where I was coming from, and I believe she eventually saw the true Roger. Who knows? Eventually, people will see the true Roger Marshall Jr.

After his binges, and after he has come down from that high, most days Roger talks to me like I am a slave or someone not worthy of respect. He will either leave, stay out all night, stay home smoking blunts all day, take shots of Patron, and watch the First 48. After he has gotten to the level of highness that he needs to be kind to me, this is the only time I get his attention.

Other than that, he is either on his phone, on Facebook, or watching videos on YouTube all day. He would manage to be nice to me if he needed me to go to a speaking event with him, and he really laid it on thick. He was pretending that he is so Blessed to have such a wonderful wife like me. Of course, he knows I am a good woman and wife; he only showed it in public.

I would imagine Karmai was lurking in the background watching our every post on Facebook, often fantasizing about what it would be like if I were eliminated, and if she were in my place—going to the different events with Roger. Instead of Roger and me going on trips, it would be her and Roger. Them going out to eat, looking so happy and in love.

She will soon be introduced to the real Roger Marshall Jr., or perhaps he will be introduced to the real Karmai Alexander. One has severe and chronic PTSD, a threat to himself on or off medication, and she has PTSD from Military Sexual Trauma. I do not know if she is on drugs, but before Roger and I married, his previous relationship after he divorced his second wife, the other women in Roger's life were all on drugs. I would imagine that Karmai is going to be Roger's karma if you will. Perhaps they will be each other's karma.

One thing I know is this; there is a day of reckoning with God for them both! Not only them but also for the foundation who tried everything they could do to stop me from talking about the unjust they did, based solely on what Roger told them. Of course, he played my voicemails to them. Roger told me he let them hear it. I knew this to be true because he would let my neighbor listen to them. What I cannot understand is, why they never questioned why I left the messages? I am not making excuses for the voicemails I left on Roger's phone. I have been hard on myself to allow Roger's behavior and actions to take me out of character. Someone that would not recognize the Christ in me if they heard those messages.

It is like they believe that I am some deranged, unstable woman that will go off, out of the blue, leave angry voicemail messages on his phone just because I had nothing better to do. Are people so blind, or do they just want to ignore that Roger has some major mental issues because he has a gift for gab, and is a person who can charm those they need to advance their cause?

Let us reverse this now, shall we? Let's shall! One day back in Rockwall, Texas; Roger and I had picked up London from daycare in Rowlett, Texas. She mentioned my previous boyfriend. She still called him papa. Roger got so upset that London called Earnest, my former boyfriend for eleven years, that he started cussing at me, saying that I need to get that fucking straight with London, that Earnest is not her papa. He told London, "That is not your damn papa, and do not let me hear you say that again." Roger speaking to London like that, took me by surprise. To act this way in front of a child, was beyond any understanding.

Roger would often check who liked my post on Facebook and being honest; I did the same thing later in our relationship. I guess he had been checking out the guys who were regularly "liking" my post. One day he said, "Who is this nigga always commenting and liking your post"? I said that is so and so. I asked Roger why, and his response was, he had a feeling that a couple of men wanted something more from me. There is this one man who I have been knowing for years. Roger did not like him; I told him that this man was happily married, was like a mentor to me, and helped with my spiritual growth. Again, Roger made a big deal over this man, either commenting on my posts or "liking" them.

There was another man who used to tag me in a lot of inspiration and Christian posts. Roger noticed it and told me that he did not like this man tagging me in his posts because it made him feel some type of way. I tried to explain to Roger that I do not know this man, but they were inspirational and Christian posts that encouraged people. And that it was at least forty or more people this man would always tag on his posts. To make sure I gave Roger that respect and to let him see that his feelings are valid, I never allowed any of this man's posts to be seen on my page after Roger's concerns. If he tagged me in any of them after Roger expressed how they made him feel, I would un-tag myself from the posts.

When we first moved to Georgia, I had to call my ex-husband to make sure that he lookout for our daughters because they were all in Texas, except my oldest daughter. I told Roger that I had called my ex-husband and the reason why. Roger said to me, that I do not need to talk to my ex-husband, and that my girls are grown. However, if there is anything they need, he would be communicating with my ex-husband instead of me. My latest granddaughter was born on

July 6, 2019, and I had made plans to go to Texas once my daughter Selena had the baby. I asked Roger if he was going to accompany me, and he told me that he was not. He said that they are your family, and I do not have anything or anyone to see in Texas. No harm, no foul. Once my daughter had my beautiful granddaughter Karmen, I went to Texas. I stayed in a hotel while I was there. I did not hear from Roger the few days I was there, not until I headed back to Georgia.

We talked about bringing my granddaughter London back to give Selena a break, due to the complications she was having being pregnant with Karmen. I had made it to Tyler, Texas, and Roger called. He asked me if London was with me, and I told him yes. He then said that I had better turn around and take her back to her momma because he was not raising another child. I thought to myself, so when he said he missed London so much and was telling people that he was so close to London, Roger was fake. The moment we made it back to Georgia and made it to the house, Roger raised so much hell in front of London, telling her that she was not welcome. We had to stay in a hotel because it was that bad.

He made sure that it would be uncomfortable for us. The next day we came to the house and still Roger was acting a damn fool! This time he was questioning me about where I stayed. And if I had been with my ex-husband.
Roger even took my phone, took the sim card out of my phone, and inserted in his phone to see who I had called and texted. When he saw I had called my ex-husband a couple of times, he went crazy. I told him that I was making sure that he was there for Selena, being that she just had the baby. I also called him to see if he would be able to buy some bed rails since I had just purchased some new mattresses for their bed. I told Roger I am not a cheat, and I take my marriage very seriously. I would never disrespect myself, another woman's husband, nor him.

Even when we experienced trying times in our marriage, I never reached out to an old boyfriend or ex-husband. I knew that would make things worse, and it would cause further division in our marriage. I knew it was something that would not please God, no matter how Roger treated me. There were times when the enemy was at work. I had blocked Earnest on my phone, and other guys I have dated who tried to reach out to me. I never entertained them, and it was when Roger left that I began communicating with an old boyfriend.

Even then, the few times I have done it, it did not feel right. So, I stopped communicating with him. I know that I must heal, and I have always held to my belief that I would never go back to a previous boyfriend. The same will hold true with Roger as well. I cannot see myself being subjected to the emotional, mental, and physical abuse. I am now healing from all that chaos. And the healing must take its full effect before getting serious with anyone.

The Demons I Encountered

The first time I encountered one of Roger's demons was our first Christmas together. We were not married at the time, and trust me, and I know what you are saying right about now. What, you married him anyway? Yes, I did. I thought he would change, and I felt that if I loved him enough, he would see he would not have to act the way he did.

We were at the carwash in Rockwall, Texas, and after Roger finished washing his truck, he asked me if I needed to do anything. I reminded him that I had mentioned to him that I needed to go to Wal-Mart to get some wrapping paper for London's gift that I had gotten her. It was a mini iPad. He was agitated about it and said that I had not mentioned it to him. I again tried to remind him when I told him. I could see he did not want to go, and I told him we did not have to go.

He became belligerent with me, and I kept telling him it was okay. He hurried out of the carwash, drove me to the front of the entrance at Wal-Mart, got out of the truck, came to my side, opened the door, and told me I better get out and get the wrapping paper. If I do not get out of the truck and go and get the wrapping paper, he will make a scene. I was in shock, and I could not say anything! As I had never seen a person go from being an average person to a person who seems to be out of their mind.

I got out of the truck, confused! Wondering if I should head to another exit where he could not see me and walk back to the condo. I thought to myself, "I better not do that, because he will be calling my phone or go into the store looking for me and cause a scene." After I came to my senses, I got a gift bag and some other items.

I do not even remember paying for the things I had purchased. I was playing what just happened in my head. Once I got back to the truck, Roger acted as though nothing happened. Of course, he did apologize for acting that way and blaming me for his actions. Saying we need to communicate and for me to act as though I did not want to get the wrapping paper when I knew I needed to get it.

Roger and I decided to go to Arkansas for the weekend. After I finished working, we packed our bags and headed to our hometown in Arkansas. I do not even remember the conversation we had; I remember Roger getting upset when we were about forty-five minutes to Magnolia. He was driving and said he had lost his wallet. I did not believe him, and I commented that he had said this before about him losing his wallet, and it has suddenly appeared. Well, what did I mention that for, it did not go well for me? He jammed on the breaks, and he did not care if there were other vehicles behind us. He pulled over on the side of the road and told me to get the fuck out of his truck, and I will just have to walk to Magnolia or catch a ride. I told him I was not going to get out of the truck.

So, he gets out and comes around to the passenger side, opens my door, grabs me by the arm, and pulls me out of the truck. He acted as though he was going to take off, but then I assume Roger realized he better not do that. He rolls down the window and tells me to get back in the truck. I hesitated because of past experiences when Roger is in this rage; Roger does not care how erratic he drives. Sure enough, he is cussing and driving like a fool down the highway. Finally, we make it to Magnolia.

We could not even get to where we are going before he pulls over again. Screaming and yelling at me. A Magnolia police officer pulled up and asked us if anything is wrong.

Roger tells them everything is okay and tells them his son-in-law works for the police department. They get him on the phone, and his son-in-law tries to calm him down and talk to him.

It appeared when Roger wanted to get high; he would always display this behavior. As if I have done something terrible to him. I dare not question him. Every time we came to Magnolia, he wanted to enlist my sister or her boyfriend to score him some crack. They would try to hide it from me and call him to the side as though it was only marijuana, but I am no fool. I would often ask him why they could not give him the marijuana in front of me if that were all it was. There was not a time when we did not go home to visit family in Arkansas, where I had to endure Roger's rage.

The number of times I often called him on his bull crap when he would ask my sister and her boyfriend to go and score some crack for him, he would often hop in his truck, speed out of their driveway, and leave burning rubber. Only to return to try and make me get in the truck with him and try to explain what he is going through. If I did not get in the truck with Roger, he would always make a scene.

After a while being in Georgia, Roger was pretty burned out with the position. We decided to go to Destin Florida for a few days to get away. The trip started out great. We were talking, laughing, listening to music and enjoying the ride. I just knew we were going to have a good time. As soon as we made it to Florida, there is this stretch of dark roads and warning signs, and in all honesty, I cannot tell you what happened to Roger's mood. Roger slammed on the brakes, told me to get out of the truck and walk. If I did not get out, he was going to push me out. I felt safer on the outside of that truck than I did on the inside with him. His voice changed to an evil and diabolical voice.

I got out and I started thinking to myself, "In a minute I know that something scary is going to come out of the woods and snatch me up and eat me." It did not happen though, because Roger backed up and made me get back in.

I believe I mentioned the time I did not want him to talk to my daughters about him being in jail, how angry he became. After they had left, he made a heck of a scene. He became so angry that he got my iPhone and smashed it with his foot. "This cannot be real," I was thinking to myself. I dare not say anything to him, or else the scariest person would appear. There have been so many occurrences with Roger in Rockwall, before and after we got married. I have had to get two televisions replaced and the glass mirror on the wall in the dining area. One day he threw a glass at me, I had to duck so it would not hit me in the head. The glass missed me and crashed into the wall mirror. I loved that mirror that covered the dining room wall.

That was $275.00 of wasted money. Roger replaced the cell phone. I guess he felt terrible about smashing it, so the next day he had bought me a new one. He had pawned the two televisions after I had gone to visit my sister for her birthday in Georgia before we moved here. I asked him if he wanted to go way ahead of time. He said he did not want to go.

The morning I left, he just laid in bed as though if he was in a trance. I told him goodbye, and I loved him, he did not say anything. He was just lying there with his eyes open, looking at the ceiling. I was only gone two days, and once I started on my way back to Texas, I called my daughter because I felt like something was wrong. She told me that she had gone to the condo and the televisions were gone. I tried to call Roger, and he would not pick up. It is the time that he went back to Houston and got his ex-girlfriend to get him a cell phone. I had the phone turned off on the old one since he did not answer. He had changed his phone number and got a new phone. I tried to call one of his sisters to talk to him, but she was abrasive, thinking that I had done something to Roger.

She had her nephew, who is married to Roger's daughter, call Roger. He had given them his new number. Roger's son-in-law texted back to everyone, saying that Roger was excellent and was back in Houston. A few days later, Roger had another sister contact me with him on the phone. He asked me to call him, and he gave me his number. I called him, and we talked about our issues. I wanted to know why he left and took the televisions.

Roger told me because he felt paranoid there, and he did not have any money to get to Houston, so he pawned the TVs. He said he felt as though I abandoned him, and that he was so angry. He was planning on getting two chickens and putting them in the air ducts so that we would get sick once they spoiled and we would smell this horrible smell, and would not know where it was coming from in the condo. I know! Bettye, girl, you should have left him way before now!

I had tried to reach out to his family to get an understanding of Roger's past. That was a waste of time. The family members I talked to would have me to believe they were surprised by his behavior. Some were not surprised at all. I remember when Roger had asked one of my daughters for the number for a guy, she bought marijuana from. One of my daughters gave Roger a phone number, and this is when the most defile and uncensored demons would rear their ugly heads. I would even contribute to Roger's addiction unknowingly for a while. I could not understand how Roger would be broke quickly and not have anything to show for it.

I believed that he was just buying marijuana and would even take him to get it because he would ask me to drive him. There were times when after he purchased the marijuana, we would not make it to the house. I would have to pull over in a nearby gas station, or parking area. He would get out of the truck and immediately take a puff of whatever else was in with the marijuana. I concluded that it had to be more than marijuana for anyone to want to get out of the truck to smoke it before making it back home.

In April 2020, Roger himself disclosed that he started back using crack when we lived in Rockwall. I knew it all along, as I could not find a place to park fast enough for him. If it was just marijuana.

I was scared about parking in a gas station, or down a road by an entrance to someone's business. But I did, and I quickly found out that if I asked him why he could not wait until we got home, it would be anger thrown my way. I tried so often to make up an excuse as to why I could not go with him. He always insisted, even if I had to bring my laptop to work in the truck. Roger wanted me to go everywhere with him. Fishing, going to get bait, drive him to get marijuana. It seemed that Roger was incapable of being alone. With the exception, when it was time for him to get his check at the beginning of the month.

Roger had gotten so bad with his addition that he would grow upset with me about any minor thing. Even in Rockwall, I would have to stay in a hotel, or in a hotel parking lot to get away from his anger and rage. Roger would always call me repeatedly, telling me to come back home so that we could talk.

One time I came back, Roger jumped in my car and acted as though someone had taken over his body, a madman. He had a different voice telling me that he has killed people before and that I better drive him to the atm to get him some money. Well, I did not have a choice. I mean, it was terrifying! I pulled into the Walgreens parking lot in Rockwall Texas.

He would not allow me to go into the Walgreens by myself; he went with me inside. He started talking very loud as usual, with no respect for himself or me. I saw an out to get away, and I dashed for the door. Unfortunately, he took my purse and my car. I had my cell phone in my hand. I thought about Roger having my bank card, and I immediately called the bank to try and put a stop on my bank card, before I could do this, Roger had emptied my account and took over a thousand dollars. I called the police after I got off the phone with the bank, but Roger was gone. They could not find him. The bank said they could not do anything because the correct pin was used to withdraw my money.

Roger stayed gone for a few days, and when he got back home, he handed me the money he had taken from my account, minus four hundred dollars. He said he was keeping it. I argued with him that I needed my cash; Roger got loud and aggressive. One of the neighbors called the police. And as usual, Roger would tell the officers about him having PTSD, and they would talk to him and leave. They would make sure that I was okay. There were a few times that I would cover for him, which now I realize did not help him at all. I was his enabler and allowed him to continue the madness and his addiction.

The most horrible thing that Roger has ever said to me in his many episodes of rage and anger was, "Your dead daddy fucked all of y'all, go and let your dead daddy fuck you, bitch". He said this one day after another crack binge and returning to our home. I was not speaking to Roger when he first got home, so for him to engage me in the madness, was truly one that use to play over and over in my head.

Roger came upstairs and stood over me while I was taking a nap. It startled me when I woke up, and he was standing over me with such an evil look. I asked him what he was doing. He said he came to see if I was going to sleep all day. I told him I did not know. He pretended as though he was concerned about me, but we all know that is not true. Since I did not give him the answer he was looking for, this made him angry. Making that horrible statement about my dad, and it went from that statement to him telling me I need to take off my wedding rings and give them to him. When I did not take them off, he came at me and snatched them off my finger, saying, "you better give them to me bitch. Bitch you do not deserve these rings". What kind of person would say this type of stuff? No decent human being would utter any of the grotesque languages to someone they profess to love.

I will never forget the day I hid in the garage after Roger got back home from a crack binge. When he found where I was, he locked me in the garage and began spraying insect spray in my face. When I would try to open the garage door, Roger would stop me. He wanted me to breathe in those toxic ingredients of the insect spray. Once Roger allowed me to come back in the house, he got in my face and as usual, gave me an evil look while calling me ugly bitches, and motherfuckers while spitting in my face and raising his arm with a closed fist as though he was going to hit me in the face. I moved closer to the bathroom by the kitchen to get out of his way, and he picked up a knife as though he was about to stab me with it. He stuck it in the bathroom door frame by my head and walked away.

One day while London was at school, and I do not remember the details of what transpired. Here it goes again! The name-calling, the threatening me, the demeaning me. Roger got in my face as though as if he were going to hit me.

The police were called to our home by a neighbor who heard all this madness. About three police cars pull up. While I was explaining to one of the officers, a woman police officer was walking up. She heard me tell the police officer whom I was talking to, that my granddaughter lived with us. The woman police officer said, "You have a child living here? Tell me why I should not call DCS"? My heart sank! Just know that Roger heard her say this also. After the woman officer said this, anytime Roger went out on a crack binge, came back home, and if I did not comply with his demands when things got chaotic, he would say, "I will call the police, and you know if I do, they are going to take London away." Wow! Just wow! I told him that was some evil and vindictive thinking even to say anything like this.

To be fair in this book, I started to take on those ugly characteristics early in our marriage of being vengeful. When Roger had left for Houston, I had access to his account. I was so angry, and I know this is not an excuse, so I chose to get even with him.

I paid his truck payment and insurance payment two times so that he would not have as much money as he expected.

I paid the utilities at the condo, and I also paid our cell phone bill. I did not realize that Roger had already paid for a week at an extended stay in Houston. I had not heard from Roger for a few days after he left. I remember sitting on the patio, and Roger called telling me how much he missed me, and we need to work out our marriage.

Roger wanted me to come to Houston, and I agreed after I finished my homework. Once I got to Houston, Roger laid it on me thick. He treated me in such a loving way. He talked about what he was going through and the issues we were having in our marriage. He told me that he did not want to come back to Rockwall to live because of all the bad memories. He even took me to our favorite restaurant in Houston. There were times I wanted to tell him what I had done, but I could not.

A few days of being in Houston, he called the automated line to check his account balance. He found out that he was in the negative. Roger immediately called the bank to see what was going on, the bank employee told him about all the transactions on his account. Oh, my God! Roger was furious, and I had to come clean. I expected him to be more upset than he was, but he became calm when the lady told him they would put the money back in the account. Roger had to call his finance company to have them to return one of his truck payments. He also called our wireless company to reverse the payment since his name was not on the account, they put the funds back in his bank account. What I did was stupid, and I have no excuse. Had I known that our marriage would only get worse, I would have cut my losses and forgot about Roger. However, I allowed the toxicity to continue. I realized that I had some underlying co-dependency issues. I guess Roger did not have anywhere else to go.

So, after we stayed in Houston for that week, we talked about Roger coming back to Rockwall. We trailed each other back home. It just did not feel the same; it was too much water under the bridge. It was not long after we had gotten back from Houston that Roger was back in Houston. This time, he was suicidal and taken to a mental hospital. The next time I saw Roger was when we met each other in Jackson, Mississippi. We both felt as though God had given us another chance to get our marriage right.

Roger was given a prescription for his anxiety by a physician, Roger said that it made him feel better. When we made it to Georgia and got settled in, Roger did not get his prescription filled. Instead, he tried to make a reasonable effort to go to AA meetings and listen to the gospel in the early mornings. It was not even six months being in our home that Roger's demons started to surface.

The day Roger picked up one of the veterans from the airport in Atlanta who had just graduated the program at the facility where Roger was the Director for the Atlanta chapter. It is a day I never will forget. I remember asking Roger if he wanted me to go with him. He told me no and that he would be fine. I did not call Roger to check on him, as I said I was not going to do that, but as the hours past and no Roger, I was concerned. I know that Atlanta has some of the worst traffic, but not six hours from where he would drop James Wilson off and back to the house. So, I called him about six hours later, and Roger told me that he was in traffic, that he was almost home, and my response to him was okay and be careful. Another hour had passed, surely if Roger is almost home, he should have been here. I called a second time asked him where was he, and this is when Roger's attitude changed.

Roger became belligerent on the phone and told me that I do not need to keep calling and checking upon him. After this, he hung up, and he turned off his phone. In the wee hours of the morning, I woke up, still no Roger. I called James Wilson to see if Roger was with him, and I was told

Roger was not with him. I drove to Bill's home and did not see the truck, so I came back home with this sick feeling to my stomach. Roger has fallen off the wagon again, which is what I knew in my spirit. The next morning Roger shows up telling me that since I called him and was at the exit to come home, he turned around and went and got high.

I remember telling Roger that since he had chosen to retake a bite of that apple, it will not be easy for him to stop. Roger assured me that he could do it, and he would give me his bank card so that he would not have access to his money. Which lasted about two weeks, and from that point on, it had been a struggle, unbearable at times, and downright chaotic! After this submission to temptation, the police were called to the house frequently.

So, it began! That feeling of hopelessness, despair, regret, and depression. I can recall one night where everything was fine, we had gone to bed, and it was almost midnight. It was nearly time for Roger's VA check to hit his bank account. He made sure he had a reason to leave that night. Bring up something "BettyeAnn" has said in the past that will surely get her upset. Well, talking about something I did or said in the past did not work, Roger would throw something in the air to see what would stick. I was not going to engage that night. Roger talked about me accusing him of women, and that he was not with James Wilson. Me, trying to figure out how did he get on this subject. I knew what he was doing, and when he saw that it was not working, he got up, got dressed, and left the house anyway. I knew he was headed straight for the atm first and then off to South Atlanta.

Roger was very strategic; he knew that when he left, I would be calling him and leaving angry voicemails on his phone. Yes, I did. I knew what he was doing, as well. He wanted that ammunition to use by my response to his actions when he needed to say that I am this crazy woman, and here is the proof. I never thought it would work, but those who do not know Roger or me that well, would be manipulated into actually believing I am this deranged lunatic. A woman that leaves random voicemail messages on her husband's phone because she just felt like it?

I had no idea the level of deceit and manipulation my ex-husband possessed. He is a master at it, and I could not compete with him, nor did I want to, I just wanted him to get help so that he would be a better husband, and overall a better person.

Woman to Woman

There are so many other women who have experienced the type of rage and anger from their spouses that I have. I am sure some, perhaps not to this extreme, and then some more extreme. Some never got a chance to share their story or tell anyone what they were going through. Why? Because many spouses have been murdered at the hands of their husbands who have PTSD. We hear about in the news, or we read about it.

Had God not closed this door, I could have very well been one of those women who never got the chance to tell my story. Perhaps, my family would have been shocked to find out if I would have been one of those women. In their eyes, most of my family thought Roger and I were happy together. For that matter, many people who followed us on social media. And some of those in our circle more than likely thought the same thing. I mean, you would have to be a dynamic duo to receive an "Outstanding Citizen of Georgia" from the Secretary of State. I honestly did not want to accept that award because I knew what was going on in my household.

My fellow sisters, please listen to me. If your husband has been diagnosed with combat trauma, such as PTSD/TBI, and has no thought or concern about him or his family. And have no interest in seeking real help without you trying to convince him, please for the sake of your children, and your mental health, please find a safe place for yourself and for your children.

It is draining, depressing, and it will drive you into an unhealthy mental state. To where you will start to see those ugly characteristics manifested in you.

The kids suffer. They cannot focus during school, and they grow up angry because this was the environment, they had to live in. They become dependent on drugs and alcohol to numb the chaos they endured growing up.

It will be a never-ending cycle. It was handed down from generation to generation. I am not saying that anyone should leave their husband; that choice is solely up to you. If you are coping well in this environment, more power to you. But if you are like the many women I listen to vent about the horrendous behavior of their spouses, it is up to you to do something about it.

My granddaughter London was a witness to many of Roger's horrible acts. There were times; she would sneak and call the police or record him. She would be too scared to leave me at home with Roger when it was time for her to go to school. I knew this was affecting her grades. She told me that she would be so worried about me when she was at school. Every day when I would pick her up, she would ask, "Are you and papa arguing, or is pa-pa at home and is he okay." My response most of the time was, "It will be okay, London." I just wanted her to be at ease when she got home.

London has so much wisdom to had been seven years old at the time. She could sense the friction in the air. She would be the one to try to make our home a happy place by being silly so that Roger would laugh. Many of our children or grandchildren are so much wiser than we are at times. Especially when they sense danger. She would often tell me, "Gran nee, you deserve better than that. If he loves you, he will not say those things to you or treat you the way he does". Listen to your children and grandchildren. Pay attention to their behavior.

There is one thing I will never forget. It was so wise coming from a then seven-year-old. One night I was tucking London into bed, after we said our prayers, London had tears in her eyes. I asked her why she was crying, and she says, "you know he is going to kill you if you do not leave him alone."

I did not want to accept the fact that she was correct, so I hugged her and told her everything was going to be okay. Deep down, I knew it was very possible that if I stayed in the marriage with Roger, he could very well kill me. He was capable of killing me, as he expressed it many times, and said he could get away with it.

My Road to Restoration

When I moved to Texas on February 28, 2020, in my home, and started my new position on March 6, 2010, I had only been in my job three days before I began to feel sick. Chills, unable to taste anything, fever, and, etc. I had to leave and go to the emergency room to see what was going on with me. I just knew it was not COVID-19. Since testing was so new at the beginning of March, the hospital where I had to stay for three days said I had an unknown type of pneumonia. I have had pneumonia before, and this was nothing like I remember.

The second day was worse than the previous day when I started feeling sick.

There was this beautiful young black nurse that attended to me the first night I got admitted to the hospital, and she asked me if I had a history of high blood pressure or if I was stressed out. I told her about my move here to Texas just a week ago and a bit about the things I went through with my husband. I could tell that it bothered her and that she genuinely cared. She then said to me, "Do you mind if I pray for you"? I told her, "By all means, I am a believer." I also told her about me being in Seminary pursuing my Master's in Christian Counseling. So, she kneeled beside my bed and began to pray for me. I thanked her for praying for me. It meant a lot to me. I know she did not have to do that, but God sent her to pray for me.

I was starting to feel overwhelmed. I started thinking and talking to God with tears rolling down my eyes. "God, if this is how I am going to die, alone, let Your will be done. I was told by the hospital staff that I more than likely had to stay in the hospital until the next week.

The hospital had to send my lab test to the CDC for them to determine if I had COVID-19. I told them I could not stay in the hospital that long, as I had just started a new job, and I probably would not have my job if I had to miss three days of work. Having to stay there for a few days gave me the blues even more. I had just moved to Texas, racking up credit card debt, a new one-year lease on a home, and I am about to be out of a job. It was not looking good for me.

"Please comfort my children". I was also thinking that this is going to be how my life ended. I felt defeated, knowing what my husband had done to me. He is living his "best" life with another woman, and I lose everything, including my life. I thought, "How is this even fair, God"?

It was a struggle for me, and as soon as my foot hit the floor to go and pee, I was out of breath. To think about walking six steps to the bathroom seemed as though I had run ten miles. My heart was beating so fast, and I was gasping for air every step I took. I wondered if I would drop dead on the floor, trying to go to the bathroom. It was a horrible feeling. I realized that I could have laid in that hospital bed and just gave up on life.

I was on oxygen and taking breathing treatments every four hours. The next day I felt a little better, but it was still challenging to go to the bathroom without gasping for air during each step I took. On Sunday morning, I had a male nurse come in and take my vitals. Things started to look good. My vitals were improving. He communicated to me the doctor said that if I could walk around the room a few times without getting out of breath, they would discharge me.

I prayed to God to let me walk around this room without getting out of breath when it was time for me to walk with the nurse in the room so that he could witness it. I practiced after he made this announcement to me. I was not getting out of breath the few times I walked around the room. The power of prayer! Even if it was only for the nurse to witness my improvement.

I did it! I walked around the room four times without getting out of breath. He checked my vitals while the doctor listened to my lungs and heartbeat on the monitor. Wow, technology is something else. No, I was not instantly healed. It took a few weeks for me to recover fully. But I want to thank the nurse who kneeled beside my bed and prayed for me. For that matter, I want to thank the entire Baylor, Scott & White hospital staff. They could have turned me away due to no insurance. They did not do that, and they never treated me any different than a patient with insurance.

I rarely get sick, and I know it was due to all the stress I had been experiencing with Roger's infidelity, the enormous amount of debt I had to try and maintain my living, not having a job that put me in the hospital. I believe I had taken so much in those three years that when I finally saw the light at the end of the tunnel, it was overwhelming, and my body could not handle it. Not to say that COVID-19 did not play a role in my illness, but my stress level was so high that it could have taken me out of here.

Again, ladies, if you are experiencing any stress, depression, sadness, feelings of worthlessness, due to being married or in relationship to someone who has PTSD, please seek refuge. I am not telling you to leave your spouse, but I am telling you to take care of yourself.

Why? Because you matter! And know that I am praying for every one of you.

Although my healing started in Georgia, I knew I would not entirely focus on my restoration by way of God until I moved away from Georgia. Being in that house made me very anxious, and I could not stand being there. There were many nights where I would go and spend the night with my sister so that I would not have to be in that house I shared with Roger.

That morning, when my neighbor put my car on the dolly of the Budget truck I had rented, I started to feel some relief. It was like a heavy weight that was lifted off my shoulders. I stopped at the Starbucks that morning where Roger and I frequent to get one last cup of coffee and to say goodbye to the young ladies who knew us.

When I hit four-hundred Southbound, I started shedding tears. They were mixed feelings for some reason. I started thinking about when we first moved there, and the trials we faced before we found a house to rent. The memories of some of the good times we shared and then looking ahead to a better future. Making it to Texas safe and wondering what God had in store for me. I could not wait to get to Texas, and that evening when I rolled on in, it was like a breath of fresh air. I had wanted to live in Little Elm, Texas, for a few years before moving to Georgia. Finally, it was going to be a reality.

Once I made it to Frisco, Texas, the view from Dallas Parkway was beautiful. I had never been that far down the interstate before, and there were so many new buildings and communities built. I absolutely loved driving and seeing all the buildings and businesses lit up.

The next morning, my landlord, the realtor, and I had decided to meet at the home I am now renting. I parked the Budget rental with my car hooked to it on the street close to the house and took an Uber to my daughter and her boyfriend's home. They were waiting for me to get there. They had food and adult beverages made for me. Tom is such a gentleman, and he knows how to treat my daughter.

Tom agreed to bring me back the next morning to meet the landlord and realtor so that I could get the keys and pay the first month's rent.

Tom was polite to ask if he could get out and view the home. Of course, I said yes. He walked around with the landlord to make sure everything was up to par. He made sure he knew what type of air filters I needed, and when it was time to change the house air filter, he would tell my daughter to let me know it was time.

Tom and my daughter, Shemesha, were Godsend! When I first moved into my home, they knew I was tight on funds. I was literally living off prayer, until I received my 1st paycheck. The day I got out of the hospital they came over and brought food, they went to the pharmacy, paid for, and picked up my prescriptions. They also did some other shopping. I did not know they were going to go and buy nice plush towels, sheets, bathroom mats, baskets, candles, for my home. Tom and my daughter did not only buy all this lovely stuff, but they also placed the towels beautifully in both bathrooms. I could not have done it as they did. I am so thankful for them.

All my children have been such a Blessing and so supportive. I believe the effacing of my marriage with Roger has brought my children and me so much closer. I will never forget when I went to Arkansas and drove to Wal-Mart, where my son works. When we saw each other, and the hug my son gave me was something that I really needed, and it seems as though he needed it also. He must have known that I needed that hug; we hugged each other for a long time. We took a selfie, and he kissed my forehead. I felt so secure in my son's arms as he hugged me as if he were saying, "Momma, I am your protector, and no one will ever hurt you again." I could boast about my son for days, he is amazing to me, and I love him so much.

Selena and Shauna are the loud ones, out of my children. I laugh when I think about some of their comments, they had said to me when it came to Roger leaving me. I will not repeat them here, but I can say they have their mom's back for sure. Of course, they were just talking smack; because they know their momma is a praying momma. They know their momma is a strong black woman and have seen me get back up when knocked down.

Hat's off to my children who have Blessed me beyond belief! You guys are the real MVP, and I love you so much!

I can honestly say that since I have been living here in Texas and alone, there is nothing better than waking up in the morning knowing I do not have to walk on eggshells.

It is a Blessing to cook when I want to, without someone complaining that I do not cook often, or calling my name every ten minutes when I am working. I no longer will have to worry about if today, will be the day, I will have to sleep alone because my spouse has chosen to go on a crack binge. It was constant in my mind, whether I would be eating alone or not. Or, if today will be a day where rage and anger from my spouse would consume most of the day. Will I have to seek refuge at a hotel to escape a mad man's wrath? I thank God for my peace and joy that none of those things I no longer must worry about!

Something that I was not expecting when I moved back to Texas, but nevertheless, it was God's will for me to go through it. That unknown pneumonia I wrote about earlier and was diagnosed with, that hit me like a ton of bricks. It was more of a Blessing than a curse. As I recovered from an unknown pneumonia and worked from home since the pandemic hit hard in Texas, I began my daily routine of praising God with worship music and often talking to Him.

There would be some tears, and questions I would ask God. I often listened to Dr. Tony Evans's sermons while working, especially when I finished my work for my employer.

I was eager to learn what message God had in store for me by way of Dr. Tony Evans's sermons on YouTube. I could listen to his sermons all day, and there were times when I would play them back-to-back. Those sermons gave me strength, courage, and a newness of my identity in Christ. I know most people will listen to some of those prosperity preachers, those sermons that make you feel good and entitled. Not me. The prosperity gospel is not something I believe in, nor would it benefit me.

Since I am a Seminary graduate, it is hard for me to listen to motivational speakers who come in the name of Christ. Nah, I needed to listen to sound doctrine—the uncompromised Word of God. I needed it to cut me deep so that I could bleed out that old blood and allow Christ blood to feel me up with His blood. To give me back my identity that looks more like Him. In one of Dr. Tony Evan's sermons, "Your Time Is Now," one of the statements he made, really cut me deep.

Now, I wake up every morning, looking around at my home, looking at the mirror of a wonderful lady that almost died. Has anyone ever watched the movie "A Long Kiss Goodnight"? Starring Samuel Jackson and Gina Davis. There is a scene where she is naked, and she touches her scars while looking in the mirror. She wonders where the wounds came from that covered her body. I do this often, look at my naked body in the mirror, not because I have visible scars, but I was told by my husband of how fat, ugly, and out of shape I was; that I often look at my melanin and I do not see what he saw.

I see a beautiful black strong woman that had been lied to about who she is. It takes a strong black woman to sustain the emotional and mental abuse that I went through with Roger. I did not allow his words to dictate who I am. Instead, I look around, and I thank God for the peace in my home, for Blessing me with a good-paying job, and the family that I have in my life.

Sometimes I will sit on my patio in the morning, look up at the sky just to let God know how much I love Him, and how much I appreciate Him. Then, there are times when I feel ashamed forever doubting Him and HIS love for me. When I walk around in my home, it is silence, peace, serenity, and it is love here. If you could be a fly on my wall, you would probably hear me often saying, "God, I love You so much," out loud. Or, "God, You, are so amazing to me."

After several months of having that "me" time with God and myself, only visiting friends and family from time to time, I thoroughly enjoyed going to Georgia and spending a week with my sister. After spending a week there, my oldest sister, Joyce, called me with my sister-in-law Jacquie being on the phone. They asked me about my whereabouts, and I told them I was headed back to Texas. I was talking to a divorce attorney, and what was going on with my divorce. They wanted me to take a detour to come and visit them in Arkansas, but that was not going to happen that day. I told them it would be a while before I had the chance to come there.

My sister-in-law's friend, Mark, had come to visit her, and he asked Jacquie who was she talking to on the phone. She told him that it was me. She said to me, "my friend Mark is a good God-fearing man that needs a good woman, and I would introduce him to my sister-in-law, but she is going through a divorce." I told her yes, I am, and I am not looking to jump back into that fire again. She said to me; he is not from here, Bettye, he is Jamaican. Oh, boy, Jamaican, huh! The first thing that came to my mind was, hearing what most black women I know have to say about Jamaican men. They are too possessive and overbearing. The real kicker was, "Oh, hell no, this is not "How Stella Got Her Groove Back."

Besides, it did not end too well for Terry McMillan. So, I told Jacquie that I do not mind being his friend, but I was not looking for a relationship until I properly heal from this disastrous marriage that had ended badly. I told Jacquie it was okay for her to give Mark my number, so he asked Jacquie to provide me with his number. He also wanted to see a picture of me, and my sister Joyce had one on her phone. She showed him a few of my photographs, and she sent me one of his photo's. I thought to myself, "he is a nice-looking guy." And of course, he said I was beautiful. Well, he did not lie!

Mark and I talked a little while driving back from Georgia to keep me company. He did not want to communicate that much because he wanted me to focus on my driving. As I got closer to my home, Mark would call to check on me to see if I were okay and alert.

I was, and once I made it home, I called him to let him know that I had made it home safe. I also thanked him for taking the time to call and check on me while driving back from Georgia.

It was a few days after our initial conversation that I heard from Mark. He respected my wishes, and I appreciated his circumstance.

We both were going through a divorce and have been separated from our spouses for a while. I believe we were both conflicted about talking to one another, being legally married. However, as the days past, Mark and I began to call and text one another often. Nothing serious, just checking to see what each one was doing, or how our day went.

Not that it mattered at the time, there was one conversation Mark and I had, it was about religion. I assumed since he went to church often that he was a Christian, but as we got more in-depth in the conversation, Mark told me that he wholeheartedly believes in God, and Jesus was a great man, but that was where we left it.

I thought to myself, "Even if I wanted to pursue something with Mark later, this is a deal-breaker." We do not share the same faith, so how can we be a couple? Mark believed that if he pays homage to God, that is all that matters. By not recognizing Jesus's deity rubbed me the wrong way. One night I pondered on this for a while. I knew Mark would be calling me later that night, and when he did, I texted him that I did not want to waste his time or my time, and it was best if we just break off our communication. After my text, I did not get a response from Mark. I felt as though I did the right thing.

I want to make it clear. People are entitled to serve and believe in any religion as they wish, but I am sold out to Christ. I know that when the time came, I wanted to be in a relationship with someone who shares the same faith as I do.

A few months passed without any male communication, continuing my daily routine, praying, praising, and listening to Dr. Tony Evans's sermons on YouTube. Not to mention, working, doing my homework in the evening and on the weekends. I started thinking about how judgmental I was toward Mark and thinking to myself about Roger, who profess to be a Christian, and some other men I have dated. They did not look anything like Christ, and it was enough conviction for me to realize that I should not ever judge someone based on their beliefs. Besides, I am an optimist and believe there is hope for anyone willing to listen from a Biblical perspective and an open heart to receive it.

I prayed and asked God that if I had the opportunity to apologize to Mark, I would do just that. It was June 13th, 2020, around 9:00 AM I received a friend request on Facebook from Mark, followed by a message on Messenger. Mark wrote that he missed talking to me, as I stated the same. For some reason, I missed conversing with Mark, but I decided to leave things as they were. I told him that I was getting ready to drive to Arkansas to visit Jacquie and my family.

Once I made it to Arkansas, I stopped by the liquor store and bought a bottle of wine, Kendall Jackson, Cabernet Sauvignon, to be exact. I made it over to Jacquie's home, my oldest sister Joyce was there, along with a few other people. Jacquie introduced me to her guests.

Jacquie made a phone call to Mark to let him know that I was in town and asked him to come by.

While we were sitting at the table, about an hour later, Mark comes in. He was looking so good and smelling even better. I got up from my chair and hugged him. Mark did not stay that long, as he had to go and run some errands. He said that he would return later, in which he did. While we were out sitting on the front porch, talking and laughing, Mark pulled up and stood about eight feet in front of me. He looks like a smaller version of Rick Ross. I asked Mark if he wanted to share a glass of wine with me. He took my glass and drank some of my wine. He liked the taste and stated it would go good with a nice steak. It would.

As time started to wind down, Mark said that he was about to go home. I got up and walked close to him. I believe he was waiting for me to do that. He held my hand as my cheek touched his, and he whispered to me, "you are so beautiful." Mark, Mark, Mark! And he smelled so freakin good too! I did not want to let go of his hand. He then asked me if I would like to come to his home. I was hesitant because I had drunk about two glasses of wine. So, I told him I would drive over instead of riding with him. Mark drove off, and I sat back down, reasoning in my head if I should go, and if I went, what would Mark be expecting when I got there. Of course, I knew the answer. I told my sister and Jacquie that I was not going to go to his home.

It was the wine that was tugging on me to just go to Mark's home. I allowed myself to have a level head, and the effects of the wine to recede before making the final decision. I told them I was going to Mark's, and so I did.

Mark had texted me his address, and as I made my way to his home, which took about fifteen minutes, I was talking to myself. Although you have not been in the presence of another man in almost three months besides Roger, whom I saw for a few days in April, I would not allow myself to get weak and succumb to my desires, nor Mark's.

Once I made it to Mark's driveway, I called him to let him know that I was outside. He came out and greeted me. He led me around his home and showed me around. We sat on the couch in the living room. We talked a bit, and before I knew it, Mark turned my head and asked me if he could kiss me. I said, yes. He did, and oh, boy! We stopped for a minute or two and started back. He held my back ever so tightly, and I held the back of his head ever so tightly. Whew!

Suppose I tell you that I do not ever remember being kissed so intimately and gently, as Mark kissed me. In fact, I have never in my life been kissed like that before. It scared me so bad, that I told Mark I had to go. Because I know if I would have stayed, and the way I felt when Mark kissed me, I would have done something I would have regretted. Mark did not pressure me into staying. He was a gentleman and walked me to my car. He kissed me before I got in my car and asked me to call him when I made it back to Jacquie's home.

When I made it back to Jacquie's home, my sister and nephews were shocked that I was back so soon. They thought that Mark must have tried to have sex with me, and I must have left because he was a jerk. When I told them, I had to leave Mark's house because of that kiss, and I was scared that I would have given up the goods, they laughed at me. Joyce laughed and said, "I thought I had heard it all. I have never heard anyone leaving a man's home because a kiss scared them away." Yes, sweetie, it sure did. First time for everything. It was just that powerful! My goodness!

After that, Mark and I kept in touch with each other. Like clock work, Mark would text me every morning with a good morning text, and I would always reply to his texts, "good morning." The morning text was the only thing we did for almost a month. Gradually we made it to a phone conversation during the evening. It took us a while before we talked on the phone as much as we do now. I believe we were both cautious about not allowing our feelings to get in the way of doing something to destroy a friendship.

Today, we remain friends, text, and talk daily, and as often as time permits. For now, we both are taking our time getting to know one another. Cheering one another on and bringing lots of laughter in the mix. Every so often, I will call him to ask about a Jamaican dish I want to make. He walks me through the process and let me know what ingredients I need to purchase. Of course, I cannot come close to his delicious meals! My favorite is his chicken fried rice! It is so delicious. Sometimes when we talk at night, he will tell me what he is cooking, and Mark knows if he says he is making chicken fried rice, it will irk me. He likes to tease me when he makes it because I am not there to eat some, and he knows I love his chicken fried rice.

I am enjoying our friendship because Mark and I both have our own homes, and we live in different states. We do not see each other often, and this is the best thing that could have happened for both of us. When we do see one another, it is brief. Mark will cook some of his delicious Jamaican meals and have it packaged for me as I pass through his city. While I am in town, we will talk to each other often on the phone. Mark knows that we should not spend much time with each other, as the temptation may set in, which would not honor God, and it may add confusion to our friendship.

A few of my sisters have told me to date around and not just focus on one guy. They believe dating around will eliminate the possibility of me getting too serious, and I will get hurt. I do not want to knock anyone's choices, but I am not built that way, the way God has me set up, I am not afraid of commitment. To date around is not for me. When I see someone I am interested in, enjoy talking to them, and the feeling is mutual, why not focus on what is in front of me? I see no reason to make things complicated, and perhaps the potential of hurting someone who may possess feelings for me, when I may not share those same feelings. I am too old to be dating around, and my sisters who gave me this advice are as well. At my age, I am not looking to date but enjoy the fruits of my labor with someone who shares those same sentiments.

I do not know where Mark's and my friendship will lead, but, for now, we are taking it one day at a time. We will continue our dialog on the phone, and every so often, in person.

Wherever our friendship lead's us, I pray that we will allow God to be our guide and lead us in a path that brings honor and glory to Him. I do not ever want in my life again, is another marriage like the one I had with Roger. God, please, forbid!

I can tell you this divorce has been trying. I see the light at the end of the tunnel, and the day I sign those divorce papers will be the day I give God a Holy shout!

Aside from the divorce, so far, life is fantastic! I would have never thought I would be mentally in the place I am in right now. I would not want to exchange my life and experiences with anyone. What does not kill you truly makes you stronger, and I am living proof.

Bible Verses that Helped Me Get Through the Storm

Sharing is caring, and I will share the Scriptures that helped me get through the tsunami I went through. You may come across some different ones that may bring you through, and it is okay if you allow God's Word to bring you healing, peace, and encouragement. There is nothing more important. Consistency is key. Stay constant with reading God's Word, prayer, praise, and meditation, that is. I do not know where I would be right now if it had not been for Christ. He is the only answer to all issues of life.

Every time I wanted to quit and throw in the towel, the Holy Spirit reminded me of Jesus carrying that cross, being spit on, hit, scourged, and crucified. If He bore the sins of the world, surely, I can overcome this. What is so amazing, I did not do it alone. Jesus was there with me, every step of the way.

Allow the following Scriptures to speak to your heart and take some time to meditate on what God is telling you, and what you hear.

"For I know the plans I have for you, declares the Lord, plans for welfare and not for evil, to give you a future and a hope."

Jeremiah 29:11

Commentary: this Scripture reminded me that no matter what I was feeling or facing during the dark times I experienced months ago, it was not God who did any of this to me.
The darkness came straight from the enemy.
God holds our best interest, and He wants what is best for us. A future and hope that will bring glory to Him. I am reminded that when bad things happen to us, if we allow our spirits to take over, it will glorify Him. If I focused on the bad, the hurt, and the pain, my future would have been hopeless.

"Many are the plans in the mind of a man, but it is the purpose of the Lord that will stand."

Proverbs 19:21

Commentary: Although I wanted my marriage to be successful, and flourish, those were my plans, they were not God's plans. He gave me so many revelations as to why it was not His plans.

I can say that, although my marriage was a disaster, God still allowed the failure to be used for His glory.

My experience and testimony will be utilized to bring inspiration, strength, and encouragement to the women who are in situations that are familiar to mine. A voice to the voiceless. To help them find the strength to find refuge instead of living in fear and danger.

"Before I formed you in the womb, I knew you, and before you were born, I consecrated you; I appointed you a prophet to the nations."

Jeremiah 1:5

Commentary: When God speaks on a matter. Of, who we are and our purpose, we are to take it at face value. I had to remind myself that anything I go through is for God's purpose.

He created me, and I belong to Him.

Who can write my story better than God can? Certainly not me, because I will mess things up every time, and He will have to clean it up.

I can hear Him say, "Daughter, although you chose to write this part of your story, I will disrupt this program and lead you to the story I wrote for you."

"I praise you because I am fearfully and wonderfully made; your works are wonderful,
   I know that full well."

Psalms 139:14

Commentary: There were times when the enemy wanted me to doubt that God fearfully and wonderfully created me. The lies he through Roger's hurtful words; that I was ugly, a failure, fat, and evil. I would respond with confidence, "I know who I am in Christ Jesus. I am fearfully and wonderfully made." The enemy will use people unbeknownst to them, and sometimes knowingly to plant doubt in who we are and who we belong to. If we are weak and insecure, we will believe the lies.

There were times those words hurt, especially when someone who said they loved me and would never hurt me, it was so disheartening. I felt worse for them than the words they said to me.

When someone who said they love you hurt you with their words, remember who you are.

You, child, are fearfully and wonderfully made! Receive it and believe it.

"The Lord is my rock, my fortress and my deliverer; my God is my rock, in whom I take refuge, my shield and the horn of my salvation, my stronghold."

Psalms 18:2

Commentary: I know it was God who delivered me from the snares of the enemy. It was Him that kept me covered, even during my stupidity, wanting to continue in a marriage that was almost detrimental to me. A marriage that could have very well ended my life. So, I understand why King David wrote this Psalm.

If anyone can live to testify about how God saved them, they will understand. I have thought about this many times, and to think about how God strategically kept me safe, I must praise Him!

"For we do not wrestle against flesh and blood, but against the rulers, against the authorities, against the cosmic powers over this present darkness, against the spiritual forces of evil in the heavenly places."

Ephesians 6:12

Commentary: I had to take on this mindset when I encountered Roger's demons. It was not him, but those rulers and authorities in high places ruling over him and in him.
It was as though I did not recognize the man that I knew, who would, on several occasions, get trapped and allow the prince of darkness to take over his spirit. Many times, I would pray for Roger. Especially when he was sleep.
There were times when I even allowed the prince of darkness to control my thoughts. However, I prayed every time I had the feeling of doing something to Roger. I would cry out, "God, please help me, this is not me! Take these thoughts away from me." Over, and over again, I had to repent and ask God to create a clean heart and a renewed spirit within me. Begging Him, not to allow the enemy to have me, or Roger. It was our departing of each other that gave me what I prayed for to God.
Even though, initially, it was a hard pill for me to swallow.

"For the Lord will vindicate his people and have compassion on his servants."

Psalms 135:14

Commentary: There were times I would yell, "HOW LONG LORD?" How long will it take Him to vindicate me is what I wanted to know. This man is lying on me, scandalizing my name, another woman driving and riding in the truck I have financed in my name.

Someone who is riding off my sweat and tears for an organization. How is this even fair, God?! The founder, who just tossed me to the side as if I had stolen something from him, and the other people whom I was there for, calling me for support, stabbed me in the back and turned their backs on me because they wanted my position or did not want me to have the job. Where is the justice God?

My timing is not God's timing, and this is something I must remember. People say, "forgive and pray." I do forgive them all, yet, just like King David, he needed God to vindicate him from his enemies, which is what I need.

I know that I cannot make God do anything, His will and His timing is perfect. I take comfort in knowing God will vindicate me, as His Word is not a lie. There is a lesson I learned from this: do not ever seek to vindicate yourself. It will never work out. Trust me, I tried several times, and when God is ready to prove you innocent, it shall be so.

"Finally, brothers, whatever is true, whatever is honorable, whatever is just, whatever is pure, whatever is lovely, whatever is commendable, if there is any excellence, if there is anything worthy of praise, think about these things. What you have learned and received and heard and seen in me — practice these things, and the God of peace will be with you."

Philippians 4:8-9

Commentary: Although hard to do initially, due to the horrible thoughts of betrayal, deceit, lies, and the abuse that consumed my thoughts almost 24 hours a day, it was hard to receive this Scripture. After crying out to God and letting Him know my pain, as I did not want it anymore, Philippians 4:8-9 got so much easier to put in practice. I did not want to be reminded of the negative thoughts anymore. To be honest, occasionally, I will think of somethings that happened, but I remember what is in front of me, my family who supports me, and a few awesome friends. I remind myself that I am not going back to my past, and I know for sure, my future looks so much brighter than my past ever did. I think about God's awesomeness, of how His grace and mercy gave me a chance to grab ahold of Him and find refuge.

This last Scripture is so profound and heartfelt. Indeed, every word read has been a Blessing to me. It has helped my spiritual growth tremendously. We should all know this passage of Scripture.

"The Lord is my Shepherd; I shall not want.
He makes me lie down in green pastures.
He leads me beside still waters.
He restores my soul.
He leads me in paths of righteousness
for his name's sake.
Even though I walk through the valley of the shadow of death,
I will fear no evil,
for you are with me;
your rod and your staff, they comfort me.
You prepare a table before me
in the presence of my enemies;
you anoint my head with oil;
my cup overflows.
Surely goodness and mercy shall follow me
all the days of my life,
and I shall dwell in the house of the Lord forever."

Psalms 23

Commentary: Shepherds lead, and I am His sheep.
Jesus will make sure His sheep will lack for nothing, and
sheep trust their Shepherd. For me, I knew that Jesus had to
take me away from the chaos, to a place of serenity, where it
would be only Him and I. That was the only way for Him to
restore my soul.
It did not feel good, but it was the path He chose for me to get
back right with God. Jesus' sheep are a reflection of Him, and
we cannot wander away to do what we want, or else we may
very well lose our life.
There were dark days and nights, but I had nothing to fear
because my Shepherd was always with me. Even though I did
not see Him, I knew He was there to protect me from the
darkness and evil.

When He led me to a deserted place with Him, conviction set in, and yet He comforted me. He gave me a renewed spirit and mind. His Blessings have been in abundance and continue to this day. One day soon, my enemies will see what God has prepared for me, and why He allowed me to go through the shadows of darkness and death. It was for His purpose and His glory! All the days of my life, God will be glorified in me and through me. No turning back!

LESSONS LEARNED

As we maneuver our way through life, we will take some blows, and we will fall, we will get frustrated, we will laugh, we will cry, and even get depressed. We will lose friends and even family members. We will fail and gain. There will be times when we will want to throw in the towel and say, "God, just come and get me. Life is just too hard for me." People say, "life is what you make it." They say, "you determine your destiny." I beg to differ. Life is all about living out our purpose. The purpose that God planned for each one of us before the beginning of time. Let me rephrase that statement. Those who are called for His purpose, who have given their life to Him, must be used as vessels for His glory. I have tried to determine my destiny, and it does not work. Only when I am in alignment with His will, it is when I see the manifestation of my prayers.

I have learned that when you see the red flags, just stop. Do not proceed with caution, and do not even bother to go with it. Stop and think about how it will impact your life and the lives of others around you. It is just not worth the risk.

I have learned that I need to love myself first before I can love anyone else.

If I had truly loved myself, I would not have gone through the chaos in my marriage. The marriage would not have taken place at all.

I have learned never to keep my mouth shut about things that matter and having a voice could save someone's life. Not everyone will believe you, but someone will, and that someone will help you to be a voice for the voiceless.

I have learned that you cannot depend on people to hold your best interest or care about what is right. So, you must be mindful of who you talk to in confidence and those who have a hidden agenda. Those who claim to be your friend. There is a lady, and I will not mention her name. We used to talk often about what happened with my experience with Roger. She told me that she could never work for the organization that did this to me. I found out last year, that she was indeed working for the organization. There are people who are only loyal to money, they are not loyal to righteousness.

I even attempted to talk with one our mutual Pastor friend from North Carolina. He had heard Roger's rage on the phone, but since he worked for the organization as well, he told me he did not want to hear anything. This was not his position a month or so prior to him communicating this to me. He knew Roger had a device on my phone, and Roger knew who I was communicating with. This Pastor messaged me to let me know that I need to be careful of what I say on my phone because Roger had called him about a conversation we had. It was a conversation about a video I had posted on FB, about a woman prophet.

I have learned that people care more about money, power, and prestige than people's emotional and mental health. If people can benefit from the declining mental and emotional state of others, so long as it makes them money, gain power, or a position, people will turn a blind eye.

There is a Mayor of a small city in Georgia who did believe me. I will not mention his name, but when I confided in him, he thanked me for telling him my story. I quote him, "Bettye, you just confirmed what The Holy Spirit had already told me about your husband. I will be praying for you and that situation." He was not concerned about money, nor being a part of the organization. He was concerned about his reputation, and what it would have cost him, had he gotten too entangled with Roger and the organization.

I have also learned that placing my trust in God, letting go, and letting Him, was the best decision I made throughout this ordeal. I could not be trusted, due to my mental and emotional state.

So, if you find yourself emotionally and mentally unstable, and want to take matters in your own hand, be still. Jeremiah 17:9 tells us that our heart is deceitful, desperately sick.[7] Our hearts are not to be trusted when we are emotionally and mentally unstable. We must give our hearts to God, and He will do what is right.

I have learned to let go of anything, and especially a man who has no desire to treat me with love, respect, and honor. To not hold on to him when the love, respect, and honesty are not returned. I have more than likely allowed this to block my view and Blessing of someone who will be happy to reciprocate what I provide.

Lastly, but not all-inclusive, I have learned not to allow anyone to drag me down where I have gotten out of character and the will of God. People are just not worth losing who you are in Christ Jesus. They are not worth you, losing your identity.

---

[7] ESV Study Bible, Wheaton, IL: Crossway, 2011

A MESSAGE TO ROGER MARSHALL JR.

With all sincerity, and it is my prayer that what has been written proceeding this, that you will receive it in the matchless name of Yeshua HaMashiach.

I do not know if you realize what is inside of you, and if you continue to allow it to use you, it will not only destroy anything or anyone close to you, but it will certainly destroy you. There is hope though, and it is going to require you to take some action.

Look within self, this is what I had to do. I asked God to show me, me, and to take out anything that was not pleasing to Him. Ask God to show you, you, and address those internal issues that are going to devour you, and anyone close to you, if not addressed.

Seek the truth and acknowledge the truth. Do not continue the path of a lie. Tell the truth about who you are and what you have done. Expose yourself so that God can reconcile you back to Him. I know you believe what you have done is right in your own eyes, and you justified it with lies, but as Scripture tells us in Proverbs 19:9, A false witness will not go unpunished, and he who breathes out lies will perish. However, if you are indeed a child of God you will profess what the Apostle John tells us in 1 John 1:9, If we confess our sins, he is faithful and just to forgive us our sins and cleanse us from all unrighteousness. Being exposed is something hard for us to do, but when we see the works that God will do when we expose ourselves to Him, we are going to forever praise Him in spirit and truth.

Lastly, I want you to know that I did not write this book to seek vengeance. I did it in hopes that it will help others understand what so many spouses go through. After all, I was with you on numerous occasions when several spouses called you to talk about the issues they were having with their husbands.

I wrote it to tell my story and break free from holding all of this on the inside of me. To become liberated from it all!

I wrote it in hopes that I can advocate for other women who face similar battles and be a voice to those who are voiceless.

To begin raising funds for a facility for women and children who need a way of escape from danger. To provide them with what was not afforded to me in my time of distress, financial hardship, and abandonment.

I pray that God will be able to use you for His glory truthfully, and not that of your own. I am not sure why to this day, there may be hope for you. It is hard for a narcissist to change. It is who you are and this is the hard truth, but I still want to have that glimmer of hope that you will realize you need serious help and get the help that you need to become whole.

I was astonished at the number of women who wanted to come back into your life, after they knew you and I were no longer together. They experienced what I experienced by your hands, and some worse. Perhaps I can understand why they would want to, and that is because they saw a false narrative with you and me. They saw us living the "good life", and at times you appeared to display positive characteristics on photos, but they did not see what I saw and experienced on a regular basis.

I was further taken a back that you, yourself went right into another relationship while living as husband and wife. You are also very co-dependent with various vices, and I pray that you will take some time to get to know you. It was not six months that you and Karmai were in turmoil with one another, and this is so ridiculous. I know I am preaching to the choir, and you have stated to me the number of Christian programs you have been in, and yet, no change. God help your soul! It is truly what I pray for.

I do not know if you remember the dream I had about the giant green snake. I do know it swallowed someone up, and this was right before you came into my life. It was a snake who deceived Eve. Most say it is a warning due to the nature of them. What we call people when they lie, deceive or may cause us harm. We call them snakes. Some say it is something that is a warning of a fear that I will have to face. Or else, it will consume me. This is my interpretation of the dream. I almost allowed the marriage, the lies, deceit, and back-stabbing consume me.

God had another plan. What almost consumed me, God has given me the strength to face it. He knows that my story will be used for His glory! I really love Proverbs 19:21, "Many are the plans in the mind of a man, but it is the purpose of the LORD that will stand." The devil tried to take me out by using you, but God's purpose for my life cannot be usurped by you, or anyone else who believe they have the power to do so.

Being that PTSD is such a touchy subject, and it is somewhat forbidden to talk about someone who is diagnosed with PTSD. I am sure I am going to receive backlash from this book, especially from those who are just like my ex-husband. Someone who covets their unhealthy characteristics and do-not seek real help, but just enough to camouflage what lies underneath. I have watched my ex-husband manipulate his counselor, and others. He would tell them what he needed to say and what he knew they wanted to hear. He does this so it will seem as though he is getting better with his PTSD and in our marriage when we would go to a professional counselor.

I do not know if they were just going with the flow to get in with the organization, or to continue to take Roger's money to listen to him talk about himself. Again, some people are not in their positions to truly help others, they are in it for the money and how it will benefit them.

I pray that greed and opportunity will cease, and organizations who advocate and assist veterans and their spouses will re-evaluate their practices. There is so many things that are broken, to include some things I did not go into great detail about, and some things need to be addressed. It is hard to be brutally honest, again, it is not cool to criticize veterans who have given up and risked their lives for their country. I acknowledge and I am fully aware of the sacrifices they made.

I am also aware of the damage PTSD does to families, spouses, and the children. Unrepairable damage. Especially the children. Think about that for a minute. A thriving child at one time has been subjected to harsh and dangerous treatment from one of their parent's PTSD. The rage and anger they see or endure. The alcohol and drug use they see. The life-threatening situations they experience. The domestic violence they see. What about the spouse, and what about the children? We/They matter too!

I pray that God's will, and it is the will where I will operate a facility that will fulfill its purpose in the lives that are depending on real hope and change. I have written the program, and if afforded the opportunity, there will be much healing and success stories to come, and God will get the glory.

May God Bless us all, and may God give you all a willing spirit to live life with a purpose.